March 201

Bartley James

Praise for *Wealth Creation*

"Bart effectively illustrates that neither unprincipled opportunism nor endless regulation can lead to business success and societal well-being. Instead, such universal benefits can derive only from a relentless focus on creating real long-term value."

—Charles G. Koch, Chairman of the Board
and CEO, Koch Industries, Inc.

"This book is for investors, but public policy makers take note. Its message for both is that wealth is created from within, not top down or outside in. For investors there are practical guidelines to identify firms early in their life cycle that demonstrate a high capacity for innovation and integrity, and that listen to and serve their customers. Policy makers must nurture this business environment for all to prosper."

—Vernon L. Smith, Economic Science Institute,
Chapman University, Nobel Laureate in
Economics 2002

"We use the life-cycle framework explained in Bart Madden's book as the linchpin for analyzing companies and diversifying clients' portfolios. A life-cycle lens by which to better understand how business firms create wealth also leads to much-needed insights about the benefits to society from free-market capitalism. Such understanding is an essential pillar for preserving individual freedom and promoting progress. Before voting for leaders in Washington, we should quiz them on how well they understand the principles laid out in *Wealth Creation*."

—Christopher C. Faber, Founder, IronBridge
Capital Management LLC

"An imaginative manuscript that integrates a dynamic approach to business systems with the fundamentals of wealth creation."

—Douglass C. North, Nobel Laureate in Economics 1993

"This enlightening book helps the reader understand what is needed to get a free-market economy to function ideally, and identifies significant shortcomings in current arrangements. Particularly illuminating is the emphasis on absence of incentives for management to focus on long-term performance of the firm, and failure of directors to provide effective oversight."

—William J. Baumol, Academic Director, Berkley Center
for Entrepreneurial Studies, New York University; author
of *The Free-Market Innovation Machine: Analyzing the
Growth Miracle of Capitalism*

"Bart Madden has packed this work with nuggets of brilliant insight. In particular, his incisive critique of modern corporate governance and his urgent call for a new governance paradigm focused on long-term wealth creation strike at the heart of what ails corporate America. Unlike the typical business commentator, Madden doesn't stop at describing the disease; he offers a provocative and powerfully compelling antidote in his prescription of board-led Shareholder Value Reviews. Madden's talent for describing abstract valuation concepts with simple elegance makes this book at once enlightening to seasoned investment professionals, yet readily accessible to curious individual investors."

—Ralph V. Whitworth, Principal, Relational Investors LLC

"Beginning with the intriguing question of how we know what we think we know, Bart Madden builds an impressive framework in *Wealth Creation* for helping us understand how economic wealth is created over time. He accomplishes this by viewing our business landscape from a systems mindset that illustrates the benefits of competition focused on delivering the highest value to consumers. His competitive life-cycle model provides extraordinary insight into the successes and failures of companies. Among his solutions for boosting business productivity are lean management practices and improvements in corporate governance. In the end, Madden's integrative work is a skillfully written book, full of interesting and often unexpected ideas for building wealth."

—Keith M. Howe, Scholl Professor of Finance, Kellstadt
Graduate School of Business, DePaul University

"An important point in *Wealth Creation* is that knowledge growth and wealth creation are two sides of the same coin. Madden's focus on a systems mindset shows the value of a firm's culture geared to fast and effective thinking processes. As the many company examples demonstrate, the extent to which a firm's employees join together for continual learning as to how best to serve customers and stakeholders ultimately determines how well shareholders do over the long term."

—Ikujiro Nonaka, Professor Emeritus, Hitotsubashi University

"Just like any living organism, a firm too will die for sure, although when and under what conditions will be difficult to predict. Bart Madden's book is a must read for those who are interested in making that prediction. Madden's competitive life-cycle framework will provide interesting insights into the historical record of wealth creation of a firm, insights that will help forecast future life-cycle patterns of economic returns that the firm will generate for its investors. I recommend this book to every long term value investor."

—Ravi Jagannathan, Chicago Mercantile Exchange/
John F. Sander Professor of Finance, Kellogg School
of Management, Northwestern University

"Bart Madden begins his book by explaining how a PAK (Perceiving–Acting–Knowing) Loop can help us to understand the fundamental process for building knowledge. This in turn leads to a systems view of the firm as an organization for building knowledge and creating wealth. His life-cycle valuation model orchestrates the handling of a firm's financial results to reveal the interplay of competition and skill, while overcoming the shortcomings of earnings-per-share growth rates and PE multiples.

Over many years, I have personally witnessed how the life-cycle valuation model has helped money managers and corporate executives deliver value-added performance that has led to substantial rewards for their clients and long-term shareholders."

—Robert E. Hendricks, Co-founder and former Managing
Partner, HOLT Value Associates, Retired Managing
Director, Credit Suisse

"Bartley J. Madden is not only a successful entrepreneur with a proven record of developing investment tools, but also a deep thinker intent on understanding the key principles for entrepreneurial success. In *Wealth Creation*, he shares his insights for a systems approach to creating and transforming knowledge into things people value. Madden recognizes that wealth is not a fixed pie, the distribution of which produces winners and losers. Rather it is something that is created—through ideas, knowledge, and action—providing benefits not only to the entrepreneur, but for consumers and employees as well.

The book brings together insights from a range of disciplines, from finance and accounting to behavioral economics and management efficiency, and will intrigue several different audiences, from budding entrepreneurs to investors, managers, and boards of directors wanting to fundamentally improve corporate governance. It should be required reading for government officials in order to help them meet their responsibilities to protect investors and consumers while not hampering innovation and economic growth. Madden presents compelling arguments that appropriate regulation—which provides for feedback and learning and respects the efficiencies that emerge when people are free to act to meet their needs—can help stave off future financial crises."

—Susan E. Dudley, Director, George Washington University
Regulatory Studies Program, Research Professor, Trachtenberg
School of Public Policy and Public Administration, Former
Administrator, Office of Information & Regulatory Affairs,
Office of Management & Budget

Wealth Creation

Founded in 1807, John Wiley & Sons is the oldest independent publishing company in the United States. With offices in North America, Europe, Australia and Asia, Wiley is globally committed to developing and marketing print and electronic products and services for our customers' professional and personal knowledge and understanding.

The Wiley Finance series contains books written specifically for finance and investment professionals as well as sophisticated individual investors and their financial advisors. Book topics range from portfolio management to e-commerce, risk management, financial engineering, valuation and financial instrument analysis, as well as much more.

For a list of available titles, visit our Web site at www.WileyFinance.com.

Wealth Creation

*A Systems Mindset for Building
and Investing in Businesses
for the Long Term*

BARTLEY J. MADDEN

John Wiley & Sons, Inc.

Published by John Wiley & Sons, Inc., Hoboken, New Jersey.

Published simultaneously in Canada.

For general information on our other products and services or for technical support, please contact our Customer Care Department within the United States at (800) 762-2974, outside the United States at (317) 572-3993 or fax (317) 572-4002.

Wiley also publishes its books in a variety of electronic formats. Some content that appears in print may not be available in electronic books. For more information about Wiley products, visit our web site at www.wiley.com.

Library of Congress Cataloging-in-Publication Data:

Madden, Bartley J.
    Wealth creation : a systems mindset for building and investing in businesses for the long term / Bartley J. Madden.
        p.   cm.—(Wiley finance series)
    Includes bibliographical references and index.
    ISBN 978-0-470-48868-3 (cloth)
        1. Profit. 2. Corporate profits. 3. Corporations—Valuation. 4. Business enterprises—Valuation. 5. Investments. I. Title.
    HG4028.P7M33 2010
    658.15'2—dc22

                                                            2009035136

Printed in the United States of America

10 9 8 7 6 5 4 3 2 1

In celebration of my wife, Maricela, and children, Gregory, Jeffrey, Miranda, and Lucinda.

Contents

Preface   xi

Acknowledgments   xvii

CHAPTER 1

A Systems Mindset   1

How We Know What We Think We Know   2

The PAK (Perceiving-Acting-Knowing) Loop   3

Purposes   3

Perceptions   4

Cause and Effect   6

Actions and Consequences   7

Feedback   8

Knowledge Base   9

Examples of Systems Thinking and Problem Solving   10

High-Reliability Organizations   10

Eli Goldratt, Business Theorist   12

Colonel John Boyd, Military Theorist   14

Correlation, Causality, and Control Systems   15

Summary of Key Ideas   17

CHAPTER 2

The Wealth-Creation System   19

The Perception of Free-Market Capitalism   20

The Housing and Credit Crisis of 2008–2009   21

Government Regulation and Unknown Risks   25

The Standard of Living   28

Summary of Key Ideas   33

CHAPTER 3

The Ideal Free-Market System   35

Components of a Free-Market System   36

Consumer Wealth, Producer Wealth, and Competition   39

Efficiently Providing What Consumers Want   41
Summary of Key Ideas   43

CHAPTER 4

The Competitive Life-Cycle View of the Firm   45
Competitive Life-Cycle Framework   45
Firms' Competitive Life Cycles and Dynamism   47
Company Examples   51
   Eastman Kodak   53
   IBM   55
   Digital Equipment   58
   Apple   59
   Bethlehem Steel   62
   Nucor   63
   Kmart   67
   Medtronic   69
   Walgreen Company   71
   Donaldson Company   73
Life-Cycle Observations   75
Summary of Key Ideas   76

CHAPTER 5

The Life-Cycle Valuation Model as a Total System   79
Efficient Markets versus Behavioral Finance   80
Valuation Model Principles   81
Measurement Units   86
Forward-Looking, Market-Derived Discount Rates   89
Problems with CAPM Cost of Capital   91
Improving the Valuation Process   93
Investor Expectations: The Wal-Mart Example   96
Critical Accounting Issues   99
Reply to Critics   102
Summary of Key Ideas   104

CHAPTER 6

Business Firms as Lean, Value-Added Systems   107
Lean Thinking and PAK Loop Components   108
   Knowledge Base   108
   Purposes   111
   Perceptions   113
   Cause and Effect   114

Actions and Consequences 115
Feedback 116
A Lean Transformation Example: Danaher 118
Summary of Key Ideas 121

CHAPTER 7
Corporate Governance **123**
A Systems View for Corporate Governance 123
Corporate Governance Needs Repair 124
A Standard of Performance for Boards 127
A Successful Cultural Transformation Example: Eisai Co., Ltd. 128
Shareholder Value Review 130
Valuation Model Selection 133
Value-Relevant Track Records 135
Business Unit Analyses 137
Reply to SVR Objections 138
SVR as an Evolutionary Process 140
Summary of Key Ideas 141

CHAPTER 8
Concluding Thoughts **143**
Benefits for Public Policy Makers 144
Benefits for Business Managers 146
Benefits for Investors 148

Notes **153**

References **159**

About the Author **167**

Index **169**

Preface

Investors searching for companies whose future profitability will far exceed that implied in current stock prices, business owners and managers seeking to improve their companies' performance, and politicians crafting legislation to advance economic growth—all use a *wealth-creation* conceptual framework, whether they realize it or not.

This book deals with ways of thinking about the complex dynamics of wealth generation and demonstrates the practical benefits to be gained from upgrading one's wealth-creation conceptual framework. There are six core ideas:

1. A systems mindset focuses not on pieces of a system, but on how the pieces work together to achieve the system's purpose. The systems way of thinking helps one to avoid taking actions that bring unintended bad consequences, and instead encourages taking actions that produce favorable results.
2. Economic systems—the rules and relationships that exist to create wealth by delivering value to customers—are devilishly complex, and therefore solving economic problems requires extensive knowledge. Seen in this light, knowledge growth and wealth creation are two sides of the same coin.
3. A prerequisite to making better investment decisions and business judgments is an improved understanding of how wealth is created. The competitive life-cycle framework is an effective way to better understand the relationship between business firms' performance and stock prices.
4. A deeper understanding of business firms makes it plain that customers, employees, and shareholders have mutual, long-term interests. In other words, a free-market system geared to serving customers through competition is a system in which participants ("society") benefit from the wealth that is jointly created.
5. There is a huge opportunity for sustained, higher economic growth through voluntary initiatives by the private sector. One initiative is to

accelerate implementation of lean management, which was pioneered by Toyota. This is a systems approach that continually purges waste and optimizes the use of resources in delivering value to customers.

6. The other initiative is to improve corporate governance. The wealth-creation principles discussed in this book offer a blueprint for boards of directors to improve firms' long-term performance and the public's trust in, and support for, free-market capitalism.

These ideas have taken shape as a natural outgrowth of the two areas that occupied my professional career. First, my research on valuing business firms, which began in 1969 at Callard, Madden & Associates, was instrumental in producing the CFROI (cash-flow-return-on-investment) metric and its related life-cycle valuation model.

The work was further advanced at HOLT Value Associates, which was later acquired by Credit Suisse in 2002. Credit Suisse HOLT continues the research to improve the valuation tools and the related global database for analyzing 20,000 companies in over 60 countries. This system is used by a large number of institutional money management firms worldwide in order to make better investment decisions.

My second main area of interest was basic issues in research methodology and the even deeper issue of how one builds a knowledge base in the first place. For a long time, I have believed that inquiry into the knowing process offers promise for improving how to frame problems, select and analyze data, and formulate conclusions for taking more successful action.

I thought it useful to craft this book so that others might quickly learn about important ideas that have taken me a very long time to develop. These ideas may seem eclectic. A focus on any one chapter in this book might suggest that the book should be classified as human behavior/psychology, business management, economics, or investments. Note that books in these various disciplines invariably promote widely different ways of thinking. In contrast, I explain a knowing process and a systems mindset in a highly practical way that provides a core thinking template with universal application.

Chapter 1 focuses on cause and effect—within the context of individuals intent on achieving their purposes, perceiving the world, encountering problems, attempting to make sense of situations, making mistakes, learning, and improving their knowledge base. Such study of cause and effect leads one from a simplistic, linear view to a concern for the interconnections among multiple variables and to a systems mindset.

Chapter 2 lays out the key reasons why some people conclude that free-market capitalism needs to be supervised by a strong dose of government regulation. This is counterbalanced by a discussion of the enormous benefits provided by a market-based economy.

The ideal free-market system does not favor large corporations, as is often depicted by the media. On the contrary, such a system has a variety of functions, detailed in Chapter 3, that support competition in achieving its main objective—value to consumers.

Chapter 4 deals with the real action in wealth creation, which takes place at the level of business firms. A competitive life-cycle framework connects an individual firm's financial performance to its historical stock prices in an insightful and intuitive way. The long-term histories of 10 sample companies are presented with highlights of key issues from the perspective of this framework. Track records for IBM, Digital Equipment, Apple, and other companies illustrate that financial performance translated into life-cycle variables greatly helps to explain levels and changes in stock prices over the long term.

Chapter 5 provides an overview of the 40-year development of the life-cycle valuation model and related data displays, and contrasts this with mainstream finance research and thought. Chapter 5 is not for you if you are unfamiliar with discounted cash flow valuation issues. If so, it can be skipped because it is not essential for understanding the other chapters.

The life-cycle model uses a systems approach wherein all variables are expressed as inflation-adjusted (real) numbers. The assignment of a cost of capital, or discount rate, is dependent on the procedures used to forecast a firm's long-term, net cash receipt stream. Of paramount importance is the continual improvement of calculations used to construct life-cycle track records, including an estimate of firms' economic returns, which leads to improved estimates of the rate at which firms' financial performance "fades" toward the average level. One measure of progress is closer tracking of "warranted" values versus actual stock prices, over time, for a large universe of global companies.

Chapter 6 is certainly for the general reader, and here is why. The Toyota production system started the "lean" revolution, the objective of which is the elimination of all waste in providing greater value to the end customer.

Many firms claim to be lean, but few have made a full commitment to lean principles at all levels of the firm—from frontline employees to top management and the board of directors. A deep probing of lean management shows not only the difficulty in sustaining a lean organization but also the competitive advantage of being lean. A knowledge-building perspective is used in Chapter 6 to explain lean concepts, including an overview of the remarkable performance of Danaher, a preeminent lean company.

Clearly, boards of directors have been asleep at the wheel in many high-profile bankruptcies—Enron, WorldCom, and Lehman Brothers, to name just three. In my opinion, boards in general lack an insightful wealth-creation framework for orchestrating the fulfillment of their oversight responsibilities. Chapter 7 shows how the life-cycle framework is ideally suited to be the foundation for a proposed Shareholder Value Review that boards would provide to shareholders in firms' annual reports. This has the potential to substantially improve corporate governance, thereby reducing the clamor for government to further extend its regulatory reach and grip on the private sector.

Chapter 8 contains summarizing and concluding thoughts on how a systems mindset can benefit public policymakers, business managers, and investors. Included are some predictions of what corporations could expect from implementation of the Shareholder Value Review.

The overarching lesson in these chapters is that a systems mindset helps produce insightful answers to important questions. Here are just a few of the questions answered in this book:

- Why are institutions and the cultures that create them important to wealth creation?
- In analyzing business firm performance, what are the unique advantages of using the competitive life-cycle view?
- Why has a 40-year commercial research program led to widely accepted valuation practices (including cost of capital estimates) that differ sharply from mainstream finance procedures?
- Lean thinking, epitomized by the Toyota Production System, has demonstrated extraordinary productivity. Why is it so effective, and why has this process proven so difficult to duplicate?
- How might boards, managements, and investors participate in the evolution of a new accounting system that incorporates intangible assets, including human capital?

Readers who quickly skim the following eight chapters might well conclude that an especially diverse group of topics is presented. To clarify, the common thread is a systems mindset for understanding the complexities of market systems and the role of business firms in creating wealth. Such a mindset focuses one's attention on the underlying processes and related incentives that drive the overall system results, and most especially, on the importance of continual firm-wide learning to improve those processes.

Acknowledgments

I had many productive arguments and enjoyable times with my early partner, Chuck Callard. His enthusiasm for research was a magnet that attracted very smart people to work at Callard, Madden & Associates, as well as money manager clients willing to support basic research on valuation. Bob Hendricks played a vital role at Callard, Madden & Associates and later as managing partner of HOLT Value Associates. Bob kept everyone's eyes on delivering research insights and developing practical tools for our institutional money manager clients. Marvin Lipson made significant contributions in the area of computer programming and database management. Rawley Thomas was a key researcher at HOLT and now leads PDDARI (Practitioner Demand Driven Academic Research Initiative), which is a unique research network sponsored by the Financial Management Association. Today, Tim Bixler of Credit Suisse HOLT ably orchestrates the continued development and marketing of the CFROI life-cycle framework.

In 1999, Chris Faber started up a money management subsidiary at HOLT that later became Ironbridge Capital Management, LP. Under Chris's leadership, Ironbridge has developed a unique, disciplined process to implement the CFROI framework. The stellar long-term investment returns of Ironbridge funds demonstrate the practical value to investors of the concepts explained in Chapters 4 and 5. My younger son, Jeff, a fund manager at Ironbridge, and I have had many useful debates about the application of the CFROI framework. Sam Eddins, Director of Research at Ironbridge, made major contributions to the CFROI framework while a partner at HOLT.

My economist friends at George Mason University, Tyler Cowen, Dan Houser, and Alex Tabarrok, provided helpful criticism, as did Jack Cohen, Alexander McCobin, and Elliott Rubenstein. In addition, I made substantial improvements to every chapter due to detailed and insightful comments from Joe Bast, Tom Hillman, and Mike McConnell.

Sara Benson crafted the figures in the book and kept her sense of humor as I made endless revisions. Kevin Reher compiled historical company data. Donn DeMuro programmed the company track record displays and has assisted my research efforts for many years. Marie Murray, formerly a journalism professor, is a superb editor and significantly improved the writing in every chapter, plus in many other articles of mine over the past two decades.

Since the mid-1980s, Ernie Welker, formerly Director of Research and Education at the American Institute for Economic Research, has been my primary research colleague and critic. This book has benefited enormously from his expertise in economics, scientific writing, and the deeper issues of the knowing process discussed in Chapter 1.

Wealth Creation

CHAPTER 1

A Systems Mindset

Like all systems, the complex system is an interlocking structure of feedback loops . . . . This loop structure surrounds all decisions public or private, conscious or unconscious. The processes of man and nature, of psychology and physics, of medicine and engineering all fall within this structure.

—Jay W. Forrester, *Urban Dynamics*

Each transaction of living involves numerous capacities and aspects of man's nature which operate together. Each occasion of life can occur only through an environment, is imbued with some purpose, requires action of some kind, and the registration of the consequences of action. Every action is based upon some awareness or perception which in turn is determined by the assumptions brought to the occasion. These assumptions are in turn determined by past experience. All of these processes are interdependent. No one process could function without the others.

—Hadley Cantril, *The "Why" of Man's Experience*

A *systems mindset* is the connecting thread for the wealth-creation issues covered in this book. This chapter briefly covers the intellectual foundation underlying the systems mindset. We begin with an examination of the knowing process, the foundation for the systems mindset. Normally, we give no thought to how we know what we think we know. That is because in much of everyday life we take for granted the knowledge we use to guide our actions in order to achieve our purposes. A lot of the time we work on autopilot, as when we drive to work or tie our shoes. We don't have to think it through each time. So why invest time in exploring the esoteric topic of how we know what we think we know? Because there can be a big payoff from learning how a systems mindset helps one to develop better solutions to important complex problems (Sterman, 2000).

HOW WE KNOW WHAT WE THINK WE KNOW

To a large extent, life consists of overcoming the problems we encounter in our attempts to achieve our purposes. Along with the easy problems in life are many enormously complex and difficult ones. These would be considerably less difficult if our notions about how the world works were more reliable.

It is comforting to have reliable knowledge to deal with problem situations that have straightforward, linear cause-and-effect relationships. For example, fixing a flashlight that no longer works by replacing the batteries poses little challenge to our knowledge of cause and effect. But, approaching complex problems with an overly simplistic linear mindset often makes matters worse instead of better.

Based on an analysis of the work of people, especially scientists, who have been extremely successful in solving complex problems, I have learned three lessons that are important to a better understanding of knowing:

1. Reality as we know it is just our perception of it—a kind of map of reality, not the true territory of reality.
2. Action is an integral part of cause-and-effect loops, with purpose playing a critical and often-overlooked role.
3. Identifying the strongly held assumptions (beliefs) that influence what we perceive and how we determine our actions in the world is vitally important to opening us up to perceiving new feedback information and to faster knowledge improvement.

Putting these lessons into practice takes conscious effort, because much of our life experience has been dealing with the outside world as independent components of reality for which one-way, or linear, cause-and-effect thinking is adequate.

THE PAK (PERCEIVING-ACTING-KNOWING) LOOP

The *perceiving-acting-knowing* system can be visualized as a loop of intimately related components. Figure 1.1 illustrates the components of this system, which I refer to as the *PAK Loop*. A useful understanding of how this system functions requires a focus on the loop as a whole and not on the components in isolation.

As noted by the psychologist Hadley Cantril in the quotation at the beginning of this chapter, perceiving, acting, and knowing is an interdependent process. Nevertheless, a discussion of the PAK Loop requires some starting point. For convenience, we will begin at the point where an individual is trying to achieve a purpose within the context of the perceived world "out there."

Purposes

Purposes are personal. They are the outcomes we, as individuals, seek from the actions we take. (This is not to say we always get what we seek.) The great bulk of our purposes are mundane. Consider all the specific, detailed purposes and related actions taken in driving to work—from as small, or low-level an action as moving the steering wheel a little to the left or right to counteract a crosswind so the car stays on our intended course. Some larger, or higher-level, purposes of driving to work would include: why you work

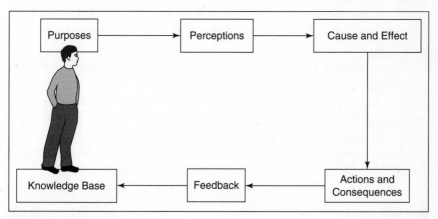

FIGURE 1.1 PAK Loop
Source: Madden (2008b).

(survival? self-fulfillment? enjoyment?) and why you have a particular job (steppingstone to a better job? prestige? power?). It quickly becomes evident that we function within a hierarchy of purposes, with higher purposes guiding, or *setting*, lower purposes.

Being cognizant of higher-level purposes is especially relevant to business wealth creation. For example, in Chapter 7 I describe the decision of a Japanese pharmaceutical company's top management to align the firm's mission statement (purpose) with the higher-order purpose of genuinely helping patients that was widely shared by employees. One result was significant improved corporate financial performance.

Studies of brain activity suggest that many of the common things we do are not associated with brain areas that are responsible for awareness or consciousness. Apparently, we operate much of the time as if on autopilot (Gazzaniga, Ivry, and Mangun, 2008). This is highly functional, and indeed necessary. Otherwise, our consciousness would be overwhelmed by minutiae—*perceptual noise*. Evolution has equipped us to do things much more quickly than we could if everything required conscious mental processing. Many actions would be impossible. Think of all the things that require virtually instantaneous "muscle memory," such as getting out of bed, walking, or typing.

But being on autopilot has its downside. Consider two economists given the task or purpose of evaluating whether minimum wage legislation is good or bad for the economy. One economist is a believer in free markets and the other believes government regulation is necessary to prevent or fix market deficiencies. Because of their core assumptions, they are on different automatic pilot programs, and their expectations are already set to a large degree (Olson, Roese, and Zanna, 1996). The data they choose to consider (and ignore), the time periods covered, and the forms of analysis employed for the lower-level research purpose of evaluating the economic impact of minimum wage legislation are most likely to be biased.

Economists (and other inquirers) who have a genuine, higher-level purpose of better understanding cause and effect need to explicitly guard against being guided by their automatic thinking and acting templates. Such researchers would be well served by, at an early stage, explicitly working creatively to overcome the heavy hand of often-unconscious beliefs.

Perceptions

Any discussion of perceptions raises the age-old philosophical question, "What is reality?" (Madden, 1991). Thinking that there is a pure, independent reality needs to be replaced with the concept that reality is actually dependent on an individual's past experience and current knowledge base, such that each of us is a participant in perceptions of what is "out there." This also helps put into practice one of the hallmark criteria of science, namely, that all knowledge is tentative and subject to revision.

In the 1940s and 1950s, Adelbert Ames Jr. and his colleagues initiated a paradigm shift away from the view of perception as a passive response to the external environment and toward the view of perception as a process actively carried out by the individual (Bamberger, 2006). Ames was frequently labeled a genius due to his path-breaking research in visual perception at the Dartmouth Eye Institute. Ames and John Dewey often exchanged ideas on Dewey's transactional approach to knowing as it related to perception (Cantril, 1960).

The Ames Demonstrations were a series of ingenious laboratory experiments that illustrated the dominating influence of observers' strongly held assumptions. For example, assumptions that floors are level, windows rectangular, bigger is closer, and the like, are particularly strong because of our extensive experience with actions being successful based on the validity of these kinds of assumptions. When an experiment falsifies a strongly held assumption, we nevertheless construct a visual "reality" that conforms to what we "know" to be true.

The Ames Demonstrations in visual perception were instrumental in showing that purpose, perception, and action are all parts of a single connected system.[1]

> [T]hese experiments . . . suggest strongly that perception is never a sure thing, never an absolute revelation of "what is." Rather, what we see is a prediction—our own personal construction designed to give us the best possible bet for carrying out our purposes in action. We make these bets on the basis of our past experience. When we have a great deal of relevant and consistent experience to relate to stimulus patterns the probability of success of our prediction (perception) as a guide to action is extremely high, and we tend to have a feeling of surety. When our experience is limited or inconsistent, the reverse holds true. . . . [P]erception is a functional affair based on action, experience and probability. The thing perceived is an inseparable part of the function of perceiving, which in turn includes all aspects of the total process of living.
>
> (Ittelson and Kilpatrick, 1951, p. 55)

The interdependent processes that contribute to visual perception are analogous to the components of the PAK Loop, which are best viewed as cross-linked together in a system that, for the most part, operates simultaneously as opposed to a mechanistic step-by-step procedure.

Cause and Effect

Problems are perceived within a given context. Attention to context increases as one's knowledge base broadens and one is able to appreciate ever-greater complexities of cause and effect. This leads to wider avenues for drawing on patterns that were adequate in the past for connecting cause to effect. Some patterns, or assumptions, have proven so reliable in the past that we take them as non-debatable truths. For example, when driving we use assumptions about the size of cars. Consequently, when approaching cars are seen as getting bigger, we also perceive them as getting closer.

Experts have more patterns to draw on than do non-experts. When past experience seems insufficient (as with a new problem), one looks for additional information (creating a new purpose) and that can lead to hypotheses about a root cause. How a problem is formulated, the initial selection of variables to study, the first hunch at possible connections, and the criteria used for evaluating the evolving hypotheses do not arise in an objective, unbiased fashion (Argyris and Schön, 1996).

In analyzing cause and effect, decision makers need to be keenly aware of the deep pull of their existing knowledge base about how the world works, which has been built up over a lifetime of experience. Also, decision makers should be attentive to the organization's culture or way of doing things that has evolved to meet a variety of purposes that, in subtle ways, may interfere with the primary goal of the organization. Culture results in strongly held assumptions that influence how problems are perceived and the extent to which hypotheses about cause and effect need testing.

Consider two examples with horrific consequences due to faulty analysis of cause and effect:

1. Will the cold temperature at liftoff cause failure of the O-ring seals for the rocket that propels the *Challenger* space shuttle?
2. Will damage from the observed foam debris at liftoff for the *Columbia* space shuttle impair reentry?

The *Columbia* Accident Investigation Board approached their work with a systems mindset. The Board concluded for both disasters that "previous political, budgetary, and policy decisions . . . impacted the Space Shuttle Program's structure, culture, and safety system . . . these in turn resulted in flawed decision-making for both accidents" (CAIB, 2003, p. 195).

That improved cause-and-effect analysis leads to better decision making, there is little doubt. But cause-and-effect analysis is not performed in isolation, even though one might, at times, believe otherwise. Rather, the analysis of cause and effect is best viewed as one component of the PAK Loop.

Actions and Consequences

The purpose of analyzing cause and effect is to learn to take actions that will yield desired consequences. As systems become more complex, so, too, does cause and effect.

Particularly in economic matters, decisions can have decidedly different near-term and long-term effects. A classic public policy example is when government officials employ an easy credit and money policy to stimulate near-term general income, output, and employment. Only sometime later do the negative effects appear in the form of rising prices and cyclical corrections of unsustainable resource allocations. A similar time delay of effects has been observed when a new CEO, noted for cost-cutting, makes large cuts in a firm's R&D budget and fires talented employees in order to improve near-term accounting earnings. But the loss of employee trust and talent reduces the firm's ability to create long-term wealth. The key point is that effects can occur with or without a time lag, or in a different physical location from the original cause, leading to erroneous conclusions about the consequences of particular actions.

Let's return to the foam debris issue that damaged the *Columbia* space shuttle to emphasize again the interrelated components of the PAK Loop. Many successful space shuttle flights, and pressure to meet flight deadlines, led to an assumption that the space shuttle was an operational vehicle and not an experimental vehicle. Within the context of being an operational vehicle, what was the consequence of earlier space shuttle liftoffs that generated foam debris? Those situations were categorized as a maintenance issue and not a flight-safety issue (Starbuck and Farjoun, 2005).

Feedback

The earlier "Purposes" section commented on the human ability to operate on autopilot, allowing us to act much more quickly than if we had to think it through each time before we could act on anything. Acting without giving sufficient thought can also have unintended negative consequences. This is so common that it is called the *law of unintended consequences*.

A key question that arises is how to promote reliability when acting to achieve intended consequences—that is, How do we do a better job of getting what we want? Importantly, we do not face an intractable tradeoff of quick, but overly simplistic thinking versus ponderously slow thinking attuned more to the complexities of situations. *On the contrary, to improve one's knowledge base, the fundamental objective should be to implement habits that promote faster and more effective cycles through the PAK Loop.* In other words, improve feedback so that evidence of consequences is accumulated more quickly and processed more rapidly, as well as more accurately.[2]

The speed and effectiveness of cycles through the PAK Loop explain both failures and successes in solving tough problems and developing breakthrough ideas for wealth-creating opportunities. These are the tasks that especially concern design firms. IDEO is generally recognized as the top design firm. IDEO was instrumental in producing the first mouse for Apple, the first laptop, the Palm V digital organizer, a needle-free vaccine, the KickStart micro-irrigation pump to help African farmers, and a long list of award-winning innovations. Tim Brown, CEO of IDEO, described how his designers work:

> Design thinking is inherently a prototyping process. Once you spot a promising idea, you build it. The prototype is typically a drawing, model, or film that describes a product, system, or service. We build these models very quickly; they're rough, ready, and not at all elegant, but they work. The goal isn't to create a close approximation of the finished product or process; the goal is to elicit feedback that helps us work through the problem we're trying to solve. In a sense, we build to think.
>
> (Brown, 2007)

Note how prototyping at IDEO accelerates feedback, leading to faster and more effective PAK Loops.

More and more companies are focusing on their internal innovation processes to leverage the successful practices of design firms such as IDEO. Employees respond enthusiastically to opportunities to deliver new products and services that are truly meaningful to customers. Apple and Medtronic, reviewed in Chapter 4, are prime examples of companies that achieve competitive advantage through innovation.

Knowledge Base

Our existing stock of knowledge affects how we perceive the world and recognize problems that interfere with achieving our purposes. We also confront anomalies that don't make sense based on our existing assumptions or theories about cause and effect. Taking actions (testing hypotheses) provides the feedback needed to complete a perceiving-acting-knowing loop.

To reiterate, the PAK Loop configuration and directional flow is a necessary construct for ease of explanation. To think of the process as a single transaction, a system with each aspect interacting simultaneously with all the others is more accurate. A market transaction may be a helpful analogy. A market transaction involves, at a point in time, a buyer, a seller, and a price, all within a constellation of potential buyers and sellers at various prices (demand and supply schedules that reflect past developments and future expectations) within an even more complex political and cultural universe. All of these aspects are captured and reflected in a single transaction. The PAK Loop captures these dynamics for building one's knowledge base, and therefore improves on the often-used (but vague) term *knowledge growth*.

Consider the enormous stock of built-up knowledge that a mechanical engineer brings to work each day. New problems without obvious answers are a way of life for engineers—as well as the rest of us. So, we experiment to try to understand cause and effect.

Given the difficulties in pinpointing cause and effect for complex systems, we *should* actively seek evidence that *disconfirms* the hypotheses we favor. But studies of how people analyze data and make conclusions strongly suggest that we tend to seek evidence that *confirms* our expectations (Heuer, 1999). Coupled with an oversimplification of cause and effect, we get stuck with bad habits that yield slow and ineffective cycles through the PAK Loop.

However, some people do especially well in overcoming this hurdle. For example, leaders of aircraft carrier crews treat their current expectations with constructive skepticism and are especially alert to potentially important new connections and alternative hypotheses.

EXAMPLES OF SYSTEMS THINKING AND PROBLEM SOLVING

Let's dig deeper into how some people achieve fast and effective PAK Loops. For reference, Figure 1.2 shows the main points about the components of a PAK Loop. This is a useful reference for analyzing how systems thinking can contribute to improved knowing and better performance in a wide variety of situations. The following examples range from organizations where exceptional high performance is the norm to individuals with expertise in business theory and in the design of fighter aircraft.

High-Reliability Organizations

In their book, *Managing the Unexpected: Assuring High Performance in an Age of Complexity,* Karl Weick and Kathleen Sutcliffe (2001) report on

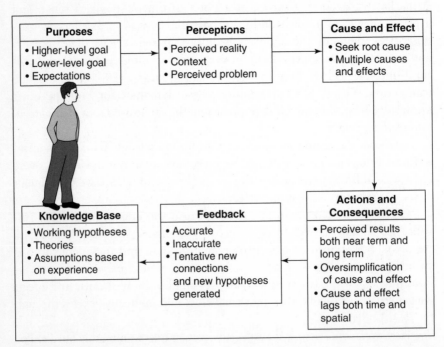

FIGURE 1.2 PAK Loop Components
Source: Madden (2008b).

high-reliability organizations—aircraft carriers, nuclear power plants, firefighting crews, and the like. Weick and Sutcliffe use the term *mindfulness* to capture the five characteristics of organizations that excel in managing the unexpected:

1. Preoccupation with failure
2. Reluctance to simplify interpretations
3. Sensitivity to operations
4. Commitment to resilience
5. Deference to expertise

These characteristics are readily explainable within the PAK Loop framework. A *preoccupation with failure* can be viewed as a purpose in itself. That is, one makes a conscious attempt to override the comfortable assumption that all is fine if no significant problems are observed. By giving considerable attention to anomalies and minor issues, mindful people continually raise penetrating questions as to whether they are observing, not an insignificant oddity, but rather the beginning of a failure in the system. Their perceptions tend to raise questions rather than provide answers because their training and experience exposes very costly negative consequences of slow cycles through the PAK Loop.

An awareness that knowledge is always incomplete and the situation being faced is always complex naturally leads to a *reluctance to simplify interpretations*. In this regard, when studying the long-term histories of firms, I repeatedly encountered firms that got into trouble because top executives assumed that the future would be a replay of their past success. This simplistic extrapolation, typically coupled to a belief that bigger is always better, was at the heart of the declines for IBM and Digital Equipment, as illustrated in Chapter 4.

A nuclear plant operator, or a crew member on the flight deck of an aircraft carrier, is trained for fast cycles through PAK Loops. Of particular importance for evaluating working hypotheses is access to real-time data. This same *sensitivity to operations* is also evident in the highly efficient Toyota manufacturing plants described as part of lean enterprise management in Chapter 6.

A *commitment to resilience* is a characteristic of those who are cognizant of, and comfortable with, their incomplete knowledge and who also put a premium on early and insightful feedback. Feedback in an organization improves as more people with diverse viewpoints (skill sets) share the available data.

Diversity plays into *deference to expertise*. Expertise is crucial to the core objective of fast and effective cycles through PAK Loops. Those with expert knowledge in problem solving need to be in charge; otherwise, performance suffers, regardless of how fast the pace of decisions and feedback.

While species evolution may be summarized as "survival of the fittest," evolution of organizational systems may be summarized as "success goes to those with faster and more effective PAK Loops relative to competitors." Building up knowledge and dealing with problems in ways consistent with the PAK Loop framework results in mindful behavior as summarized by Weick and Sutcliffe:

> [M]indfulness is essentially a preoccupation with updating. It is grounded in an understanding that knowledge and ignorance grow together. When one increases so does the other. Mindful people accept the reality of ignorance and work hard to smoke it out, knowing full well that each new answer uncovers a host of new questions. The power of a mindful orientation is that it redirects attention from the expected to the [perceived to be] irrelevant, from the confirming to the disconfirming, from the pleasant to the unpleasant, from the more certain to the less certain, from the explicit to the implicit, from the factual to the probable, and from the consensual to the contested. Mindfulness and updating counteract many of the blind spots that occur when people rely too heavily on expectations. It is these very same blind spots that conceal the early stages of eventual disruptions. And it is the removal of these blind spots that is an important part of managing the unexpected. People on carriers work hard to minimize blind spots.
>
> (Weick and Sutcliffe, 2001, p. 44)

Systems thinking can be applied to basically any problem situation. Two impressive applications are described in the following.

Eli Goldratt, Business Theorist

Eli Goldratt, a former physicist, has enormous expertise in applying systems thinking and cause-and-effect analysis to business firms in order to improve their performance. Goldratt communicates through conferences and videos (see www.eligoldratt.com) and popular novels such as *The Goal* (2004).

Goldratt's *Theory of Constraints* employs systems thinking to answer three core diagnostic and prescriptive questions:

1. What to change?
2. Change to what?
3. How to cause the change?

His thinking tools help to map complex systems, and track cause and effect attuned to pinpointing root sources of undesirable effects; identify constraints; uncover faulty assumptions; and develop, communicate, and implement solutions (Dettmer, 2007).

Goldratt begins with the goal of a system. A constraint is anything that interferes with achieving the goal. The key constraint, or bottleneck, is the largest impediment to improving system performance. Hence, the answer to the question of what to change is: Fix (elevate) the key constraint.

A key concept in Goldratt's mapping logic is the difference between local efficiency and overall system efficiency. Employees typically have expertise in one function or department within a larger organization. And their motivation is almost always to optimize productivity solely for their function or their department.

However, optimizing local efficiencies does not necessarily translate into optimizing overall system efficiency. Consider a manufacturing line where the key constraint is actually machine B. Although the installation of a more efficient and faster machine A upstream from and feeding into B will improve A's performance, this can easily make matters worse for B and degrade the overall system performance.

Another key idea is to apply constructive *skepticism to the oftentimes hidden assumptions that influence ways of thinking and doing things and that are the root causes of problems*. This is necessary to overcome misperceptions of problems. Important constraints often reside not in a physical process, but rather in the mindset of the managers (i.e., in how managers perceive reality).

Absent a systems mindset, managers can observe a resource sitting idle and reflexively conclude that this represents waste. Why? In terms of the PAK Loop, most likely their knowledge base reflects experience in improving local efficiencies as measured by accounting data.

The problem is not an idle machine, but how problems are perceived. Elimination of waste (activities that do not add value to the end customer) is critically important, as discussed in Chapter 6. Nevertheless, considerable care is needed to keep an eye on how a change in a process will impact the performance of the overall system. Goldratt provides valuable advice in terms of problem identification—look for the key constraint, which will not likely be an idle machine.

Colonel John Boyd, Military Theorist

Widely recognized as the best pilot at the Fighter Weapons School at Nellis Air Force base in the1950s, John Boyd would defeat all opponents in engagements, and typically within 40 seconds. Throughout his career, he developed practical solutions to complex problems and improved his thinking process for making decisions. His energy maneuverability theory for jet fighters was, at bedrock, a dynamic systems approach for analyzing design tradeoffs. It was critically important to the development of the hugely successful F-16 aircraft (Hammond, 2001). Corcam (2002, p. 127) described it as "fundamental and as significant to aviation as Newton was to physics."

Boyd is most remembered for his *OODA Loop*, which he first used to explain his extraordinary success in aerial combat, and which he later generalized to maneuver warfare. He contended that success in conflict depended on operating inside the opponent's *observation-orientation-decision-action* time cycle, or OODA Loop. In operation, when one takes unexpected actions at a fast tempo, this can cause opponents to slow the orientation component of their OODA Loops and breed confusion as to what action they should take. Boyd noted that the German blitzkrieg strategy in World War II was successful because it allowed freedom at the platoon level to exploit opportunities via rapid OODA Loops.

The popularity of OODA Loop thinking has spread to business managers implementing time-based strategies to gain competitive advantage (Stalk and Hout, 1990). Boyd's detailed version of the OODA Loop (see Osinga, 2007, p. 231 and also www.d-n-i-net/dni/john-r-boyd/), while not explicitly dealing with the knowledge base and purposes components of the PAK Loop, nevertheless is similar in many respects to the PAK Loop. The OODA Loop corresponds to the PAK Loop as follows: observation (perceptions), orientation (cause and effect), decision/action (actions and consequences). Both the PAK Loop and the OODA Loop operate as a system. Boyd describes this as follows:

> Note how orientation shapes observation, shapes decision, shapes action, and in turn is shaped by the feedback and other phenomena coming into our sensing or observing window. Also note how the entire "loop" (not just orientation) is an on-going many-sided implicit cross-referencing process of projection, empathy, correlation, and rejection.
>
> (John Boyd, quoted in Corcam [2002, p. 344])

CORRELATION, CAUSALITY, AND CONTROL SYSTEMS

In contrast to Boyd's OODA Loop, the PAK Loop makes explicit the importance of one's knowledge base and purposes that operate "behind the scenes" in the perception of problems. Consider steelworkers in two radically different environments. Chapter 4 contains the track records and company descriptions for both Bethlehem Steel and Nucor Corporation, another steel company. Bethlehem management was noted for an especially adversarial relationship with its unionized workforce and routinely fired large numbers of employees. Conversely, Nucor's nonunionized workforce, under its CEO Ken Iverson, was regularly paid substantial bonuses for productivity gains, participated in a culture of teamwork and respect for employees' problem-solving skills, and also benefited from a no-layoff policy.

Is it not plausible that a Bethlehem steelworker would either ignore, *or perhaps not even perceive,* a problem that would quickly gain the attention of a Nucor steelworker? In this case, their assumptions about their employer ("management exploits us" versus "management treats us fairly and respects our abilities") and employee purposes ("productivity gains are for management to worry about" versus "help those on my team to improve productivity") must certainly play an important role in how situations are perceived.

These different perceptions tie into a fundamental observation on improving the performance of organizations that was made by Steve Zaffron and Dave Logan (2009, p. 6): "How people perform correlates to how situations occur to them." In addition, assumptions about both the past and the future influence people's perception—that is, how a situation occurs to them.

Ignoring the heavy influence of assumptions in shaping employees' perceptions can easily lead management astray. That is, a faulty analysis of cause and effect leads to performance improvement initiatives that yield little, if any, sustained benefits.

An oversimplification of cause and effect is a major danger in problem solving. Note that oversimplification is a bullet point under the "Actions and Consequences" component (see Figure 1.2). Initially, it could be interpreted as the customary warning not to automatically conclude that X causes Y just because X is highly *correlated* with Y. While that is true, the key issue here is that individuals using systems thinking have the goal of gaining a more reliable knowledge base. And how one handles cause and effect is critical to achieving that goal.

Consider the situation of opening windows in a room (variable X) during a very cold winter and then observing (feeling) warm air (variable Y) beginning to flow through the vents into the room. In this case, the correlation of X with Y appears to imply that X causes Y. But, the key prerequisite to understanding this situation is to realize that a *control system* is involved. The thermostat in the room is adjusted to a desired temperature setting, or reference perception. If opening windows results in a temperature in the room significantly below the reference perception, the thermostat calls for the furnace to send warm air until the error term (actual versus reference perception) drops to zero. Room temperature is the control variable.

This shows that the degree of correlation between the independent and dependent variables depends on the environment, or context—in this case, the outside air temperature relative to the thermostat setting. The conclusion that opening windows "causes" warm air to flow through the vents ignores the purpose of the thermostat control system and yields an inaccurate understanding of the situation. The main message here is to be aware of situations that involve control systems, for such systems have a purpose and involve actions that can control perception.

A compelling case has been made that we humans have neural circuits wired as control systems.[3] As such, analyses of human behavior that ignore control variables and reference points can lead to illusions about cause and effect. Along these lines, have you not sometimes been initially puzzled by a person's observed behavior until later you learn what motivated that behavior, which is to say what his or her control variable was?

Summary of Key Ideas

■ People participate in shaping their perceived reality and are an integral part of the problems they seek to resolve. Being aware that we are unavoidably biased will help us to be open to observations and thoughts that go against our biases and could, perhaps, improve our lives.

■ Difficulty in solving a problem varies in relation to the difficulty of understanding cause and effect for the system in which the problem resides. Systems involve causal loops in which cause and effect are intertwined.

■ Excessive reliance on an analysis of variables in isolation misses the importance of system complexity, of the multiplicity of simultaneously interacting relationships, and thus often is not capable of revealing how a system, as a whole, functions. In such instances, problems are perceived within a silo, leading to actions that produce unintended, bad consequences.

■ A systems mindset facilitates a transition from observing specific events, to realizing the patterns that connect events, and to a deeper appreciation of the interactive structure of a system. Understanding system structure is the key to discovering root causes of undesirable system effects. Often, a root cause is contained in a faulty assumption that has gone undetected because its connection to one or more undesirable effects is not obvious.

■ One reason why organizations tend to encounter wickedly difficult problems is that their employees have myriad personal worldviews, purposes, and expectations. Systems involving people, who are purpose-driven, are ill-suited to simple, linear cause-and-effect analysis.

■ Instead of treating perception, action, and knowledge as independent of one another, a better method is to emphasize the close relationships among perceiving, acting, and knowing. The PAK Loop is designed to do this.

■ The benefit of a systems mindset is in developing faster and better solutions to problems. Whether problems are encountered in ecology, engineering, economics, or whatever the subject, a systems mindset helps to achieve better solutions. These are solutions that result in significant improvement to the performance of the overall system, in a cost-effective manner, while minimizing unintended adverse side effects.

CHAPTER 2

The Wealth-Creation System

*The key to building a foundation to understand the process
of economic change is beliefs—both those held by individuals
and shared beliefs that form belief systems. The explanation
is straightforward; the world we have constructed and are
trying to understand is a construction of the human mind. It
has no independent existence outside the human mind; thus
our understanding is unlike that in the physical sciences. . . .
The whole structure that makes up the foundation of human
interaction is a construct of the human mind and has evolved
over time in an incremental process; the culture of a society is the
cumulative aggregate of the surviving beliefs and institutions.*
                    —Douglass C. North, *Understanding the Process of
                                          Economic Change*

The housing and credit crisis of 2008–2009 prompted many to conclude
that greatly expanded government regulation was needed. For some, the
term *free-market capitalism* became synonymous with greed and outsized
compensation to business executives who lined their own pockets at the
expense of consumers and shareholders. In this chapter, the crisis is analyzed in order to gain a deeper appreciation for the complex issues involved,
including the design of new regulations. In addition, the impressive historical record of consumer benefits from free-market capitalism is reviewed.
This long record of wealth creation and improvement in the human condition is a necessary reminder at times, like 2008–2009, when prior excesses
and imbalances get corrected during a painful economic contraction and
when many argue for greater government control of resources.

THE PERCEPTION OF FREE-MARKET CAPITALISM

There is an elegance of automatic adjustment built into an *ideal* free-market system. Price signals and profit incentives, rewards and punishments, all work to raise a society's standard of living in a highly efficient manner. Before considering how the components of such a free-market system operate, we should briefly review five important and interrelated issues that are critical to whether a society moves toward or away from an ideal free-market system:

1. After the Reagan revolution ignited an expansion, albeit not without interruption, of economic output and business profits, there developed a trend for management to negotiate compensation structures so that management benefits mightily if short-term results are positive, but management avoids significant penalties if results sour over the long term. An extreme example is the payment of extraordinarily huge "golden parachutes" to CEOs who are fired for underperformance.

2. A system that is perceived, first and foremost, to take care of the fat cats, has a chilling effect on the public's trust in free markets and leads to demands for more government regulation. Proponents of free markets tend to underestimate this visceral effect and rationalize that the public simply needs to be better educated about the benefits of an ideal free-market system.

   A wakeup call about this was reflected in some research based on the World Values Survey data, which covers a large universe of countries. The researchers concluded that "distrust fuels support for government control over the economy . . . distrust generates demand for regulation even when people realize that the government is corrupt and ineffective; they prefer state control to unbridled activity by uncivic entrepreneurs" (Aghion, Algan, Cahuc, and Shleifer, 2009, p. 2).

3. To address perceived social needs, politicians who favor more and more government control over resources tend to automatically frame free-market capitalism as the cause of all sorts of economic ills. This includes crises that were at least partly caused by laws and regulations passed to advance politically inspired economic goals, such as homeownership. The housing and credit crisis that erupted in 2008 is complex; but certainly government had a hand, as discussed in the next section, in bringing the U.S. financial system to the verge of collapse.

4. Further, due to the lack of an insightful wealth-creation framework, far too many managements and boards of directors of publicly held corporations focus obsessively on quarterly earnings. Compounding this, corporate accounting control systems tend to promote a short-term horizon. These can easily turn into an obstacle to the continual development of employees' capabilities as well as the processes that actually result in the accounting profits.

5. For free-market capitalism to regain wide trust, business leaders need to plainly communicate to the public their commitment to its principles. Instead, the public sees massive corporate lobbying efforts that may be justified on occasion, but often amount to seeking special tax breaks and ways to undermine their competition.

In their important book, *Saving Capitalism from the Capitalists*, Rajan and Zingales (2003, p. 276) sum up the situation: "Capitalism's biggest political enemies are not the firebrand trade unionists spewing vitriol against the system but the executives in pin-striped suits extolling the virtues of competitive markets with every breath while attempting to extinguish them with every action."

This brief description of the current status of free-market capitalism paints a rather pessimistic picture. But if one focuses on the historical record of benefits delivered to all members of a society from free-market capitalism, a decidedly optimistic picture emerges.

The material presented in this book is designed to sharpen one's way of thinking about economic issues, of which the above five concerns are representative. The perspective used, which may be new for many readers, is to understand the economy via a bottom-up focus on business firms that are competing to better serve customers. That journey requires that we first gain a basic understanding of the housing and credit crisis of 2008—2009 and the criticism of free-market capitalism that it spawned.

THE HOUSING AND CREDIT CRISIS OF 2008–2009

Questions abound about the details of the timing and causes of the worldwide financial and economic crisis that first became highly visible with U.S. subprime mortgage problems. Financial innovations had increased the availability of credit for all segments of the economy and led to a robust economic expansion. To our great detriment, the increased availability of credit was taken to abusive and excessive levels. This fostered unsustainable levels of economic activity and unsustainable valuations of both financial and nonfinancial assets.

By the summer of 2007, delinquent and defaulted subprime residential mortgages had increased significantly. That raised concern that properties would be repossessed and auctioned off, and that values of the investment assets tied to them would drop sharply. Subsequent events confirmed those fears and heightened them. Clearly, the housing boom was over and severe problems were on the horizon. More immediately, it was realized that, as asset values dropped, financial firms with risk exposure to these assets would experience reductions in equity capital.

At financial firms with the greatest exposure, and at those with very high financial leverage, asset write-downs and write-offs translated into very large reductions in equity capital. Equity capital became further stressed because the high leverage reflected, in part, very short-term borrowings that needed to be repeatedly rolled over near term. Creditors of all types began to worry about getting their funds back. So, instead of rolling over the credits as would normally occur, they began to demand repayment of their funds. Creditors could not be found to replace those who wanted out. Even the giant banks and brokerage houses refused to lend to each other without getting high-quality collateral.

Troubled banks and Wall Street firms attempted to sell financial assets in order to get the funds to pay creditors that wanted out. But because the severity of credit problems was so uncertain for some firms, and by extension, for the financial sector as a whole, buyers were scarce for what were typically highly tradable (liquid) financial assets, with the exception of Treasury- or other government-guaranteed obligations.

The painful, corrective phase of the unsound extension and use of credit, and of the unsustainable boom economy and asset valuations, was underway. All of the reinforcing multipliers working between and among the financial and nonfinancial sectors that had generated large increases in macro wealth measures during the boom phase still operated once the bubble burst, but now they worked to broaden, extend, and deepen the contraction to the point that a worldwide economic collapse was feared. Widespread calls arose for governments to intervene.

The core risk management beliefs associated with the innovative products (mortgage products among them) were that credit losses would be moderated through diversification and that historical default relationships would continue in the future. Many would pay a severe penalty for these faulty beliefs.

To dig a bit deeper into the complex causes behind the credit crisis, let's begin with the assertion by many politicians that the credit crisis was due to excessive reliance on the free market and the absence of necessary regulations. A useful starting point is two organizations that played an especially noteworthy role in the credit crisis. Although Fannie Mae and Freddie Mac were publicly traded, they were originally organized by the government to advance the goal of greater homeownership. It is apparent that homeownership by lower-income people was a politically inspired goal, that is, something that politicians perceived as a worthwhile social objective and likely to help get votes in future elections. Fannie and Freddie were primary vehicles chosen to achieve that political goal.

Because the government "stood behind" Fannie and Freddie, investors considered their debt securities to be safer than those of competitors, leading to lower borrowing costs. This nearly unlimited access to lower-cost funds gave them a clear advantage over non-favored private competitors.

But the ownership structure was flawed because it interfered with a key principle of free markets —those who misjudge risk and make bad decisions should suffer the consequences. Absent this feedback component, learning does not occur and bad practices continue. With the government standing behind them, management at Fannie and Freddie put its foot on the accelerator with little regard for risk.

Then, in the early 1990s, the capital requirements for Fannie and Freddie were dramatically lowered. Fannie and Freddie entered the subprime market and management put its foot even harder on the accelerator. Keeping this machine well oiled and running were the banks and other mortgage lenders and brokers who saw a profit in making loans to people even though they were unsound credit risks because the loans had an eager buyer or guarantor in Fannie and Freddie.

Success and failure lost all reward and punishment meaning to the executives running Fannie and Freddie. When accounting profits were good, management was extremely well compensated for their "skill." When profits were not so good, management pointed out it was because they were serving the public interest by promoting homeownership.

With passage of the Federal Housing Enterprise Financial Safety and Soundness Act of 1992, Congress created a regulator for Fannie and Freddie. That regulator, the Office of Federal Housing Oversight, had to get its budget approved annually by Congress, so Fannie and Freddie made very sizable political contributions to their allies in Congress. Think of those contributions as paying tolls to travel on a road that circumvented the free-market process.

The 1995 renewal of the revised Community Reinvestment Act of 1977 pressured banks into lending to lower-income, high-risk homebuyers. With rising home prices and expanding availability of credit, accompanied by exceedingly low interest rates engineered by the Federal Reserve after the Internet bubble burst and the stock market tanked in 2002, those buying beyond their means saw only the upside of their mortgage-financed homes. Note that very low interest rates make financing homes easier and also tend to boost the prices of long-life assets such as homes. Furthermore, the 1997 Tax Act eliminated capital gains tax on a primary residence for the initial $500,000 of capital gains. A buyer could now deduct the interest on his mortgage for tax purposes while also getting a tax-free capital gain. To no surprise, home prices continued to surge.

Meanwhile, as home prices were steadily marching upward at a pace far above the historical norm, another boost came in the form of mortgage-backed securities. The inherent downside risk of mortgage-backed securities, in an environment of weak home prices, was masked by the major rating agencies, which typically awarded the highest investment-grade ratings to the top tranches of these securitized instruments. The rating agencies were arguably in a conflict-of-interest position as they earned fees from firms that both organized and sold mortgage-backed securities.

In addition, credit default swaps (CDSs) were developed to hedge the risk of a firm going bankrupt. A CDS is a contract in which the buyer makes payments (think insurance premiums) to the seller and in return receives a payment if and when an underlying financial instrument, such as a bond, defaults (think recovery for insured loss). The mind-boggling surge in the use of CDSs added enormous complexity to an already-complex financial system (Eddins, 2009). CDSs have customized terms, lack market prices and transparency, and were unregulated. AIG, Bear Stearns, Lehman Brothers, Citigroup, and other institutions that imploded were major players in the CDS market.

Financial innovations in recent times brought greatly increased risk to consumers and a lack of trust in the financial system. In this regard, John Bogle opined, ". . . innovation in the financial field has, by and large, been carried out to serve the innovators and not to serve the investors" (2009, p. 19).

Trust is dependent on the competence and the character of the party to be trusted, or not trusted. Imagine that you are a customer having to rely on someone else's performance—say on the emergency room services at a hospital. Would you not expect the hospital to have the necessary equipment, procedures, and trained staff to provide the care needed? What if they were substandard, and the care provided worsened your condition, maybe putting your life in jeopardy? What if you later learned the hospital was cutting corners because of financial stress, yet the hospital's top administrators earned outsized compensation for meeting financial performance targets? Would you not become distrustful of that hospital and hospitals in general? Would you not think that some authority should intervene to assure better service?

Competence encompasses skills and knowledge. The benefits of voluntary exchange via markets are, in part, functions of an economy's level of specialization and division of labor. But as a higher proportion of parties to exchange demonstrate incompetence, people become less willing to do business with parties whose competence they cannot quickly judge. Yet, it is easy to see that competence alone is insufficient.

Trust is tied to character. Because the importance of specialized knowledge has grown in the modern economy, more people have to rely more often on experts if general economic wellbeing is to improve. When experts employ their knowledge to serve their own narrow and immediate self-interest first and treat customers primarily as sources of revenue, not only do those specific experts deserve distrust, they also sow distrust broadly. When large numbers of customers suffer from (mis)placing their trust in experts, support of free-market institutions understandably wanes. And that's not good for free markets, or for progress. Further, as noted earlier in this chapter, lack of trust invariably leads to more government regulation. This challenge is addressed in the next section.

GOVERNMENT REGULATION AND UNKNOWN RISKS

In his (2007) book, *A Demon of Our Own Design*, Richard Bookstaber provides insights based on his decades of experience at the "center of the universe" for derivatives and risk management for major Wall Street firms. My takeaway from Bookstaber's analysis of financial risk and regulation is summarized as follows:

- Typically, innovations involving derivative instruments are introduced with little knowledge of their potential impact on the overall financial system.
- Risk management at major Wall Street firms involves a lot of detailed number crunching about known risks and past relationships of asset

prices. But big disasters lurk in the unknown risks that require extreme vigilance in order to secure an early warning and take necessary action.

- The explosion in derivatives entailed these three ingredients for a systemic market crisis:
  1. Tightly coupled markets due to high-speed information flows.
  2. Resulting higher liquidity (high volume of trading at small price differentials), which was interpreted as justification for the high levels of leverage.
  3. Enormous complexity, creating financial linkages across global markets without there necessarily being ties in economic activity.
- A regulatory structure can add more complexity and lead to greater instability. For example, when certain asset values decline, a bank could be forced to sell other assets in order to raise capital to meet regulatory requirements, which in turn drives down the prices for these assets. This then causes another regulatory demand to raise capital, and so it goes.

Bookstaber aptly summarizes his approach to the innovation-induced instability of the financial system: "Simpler financial instruments and less leverage will create a market that is more robust and survivable."

How might a regulatory framework be designed that moves the system toward simpler financial instruments and less leverage without unduly interfering with the innovation that genuinely benefits customers? Let's begin by revisiting the discussion in Chapter 1 about mindfulness within the context of the PAK Loop.

High-reliability organizations such as firefighting crews, aircraft carrier crews, and the like, practice ways of perceiving-acting-knowing predicated on extreme skepticism that the system is functioning normally. Particularly noteworthy is their preoccupation with failure and reluctance to simplify interpretations. This would seem to be the ideal behavior that regulators (and investors) would want within financial firms.

This suggests that top managements at financial firms need to share the same motivations as leaders of high-reliability organizations and be organized to generate and act quickly on information that might overturn strongly held assumptions about management's current policy on risk management. As for risk management in larger firms, Bookstaber encourages a streamlined risk management operation so that top management will "eschew pinpoint targeting of the observed risks in favor of lower-resolution, 360-degree radar that is more likely to capture the unobserved risks."

In terms of a proposal for a more reliable risk regulation framework, three points merit consideration. First, higher levels of capital should be required as financial firms use more complex products about which there is a lack of clear understanding about their effects on the overall financial system under a wide variety of circumstances. The regulatory capital requirement should adjust over time so that an innovation that benefited customers and proved "safe" over different market cycles would earn a reduction from an initially high level of required capital.

Second, a key to controlling risk is the compensation system a firm uses (Black, 2009). Many performance-based, compensation arrangements pay outsized rewards for big, short-term, profit generation—risk is rewarded. But, as a practical matter, risk is not commensurately punished when big losses hit after the annual bonuses are paid out.

One way to address this fundamental issue is for regulators to evaluate a firm's compensation system for management, and then adjust capital requirements accordingly. Lower/higher capital requirements would apply to firms in which a given year's compensation is paid out over a longer/shorter number of future years. With this arrangement, future losses due to past risky bets would reduce management's payout by the rationale that past profits were illusory.

This regulatory innovation would give Board Compensation Committees a powerful reason to go against the wishes of top executives and other key managers who prefer not to have their compensation conditional on longer-term performance. In turn, it would motivate management to do what regulators are ill-equipped to do. That is, management would pay a lot of attention to uncovering unknown risks and, as new learning takes place, adjust operating policies accordingly.

Third, lawmakers need a systems view in order to avoid legislation that could add more complex "safety" regulations but actually make matters worse. In this regard, the above approach focuses on simplicity and continuous learning in order to enable regulators to "set the dials" on capital requirements gleaned from the experience they gain over different market cycles.

In conclusion, in the aftermath of the credit crisis, which left us with widespread support for increased regulation, it is easy to lose sight of the long-term benefits of free-market capitalism over government control of resources. To regain our perspective, a good beginning point is to consider the historical record of growth in the standard of living.

THE STANDARD OF LIVING

The real goal of a society's economic system should be to raise the overall standard of living (Leeson, 2009). The enormous gains in the standard of living (see Figure 2.1) due to free-market capitalism over the past two centuries argue for preserving that which has worked so well (Baumol, 2002).

The remarkable gains in the standard of living over the past two centuries, shown in Figure 2.1, raise a question: Why did this not occur in earlier centuries? There are at least three plausible and interrelated answers to this question.

First, the components necessary for free-market capitalism to exist (discussed more fully in Chapter 3) were clearly missing in earlier centuries. Most notably missing was the freedom for people to broadly pursue their interests, which is the bedrock foundation for any meaningful economic progress.

One's interests (needs) are principally of two types. Meeting of basic material needs is roughly approximated by gross domestic product (GDP). Then there are more difficult to quantify, nonmaterial contributions to making life good. This includes, but is not limited to, meaningful relationships

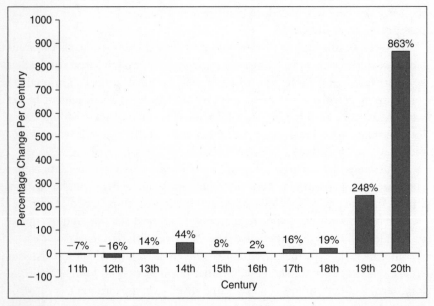

FIGURE 2.1   Growth in World Per-Capita GDP by Century
Source: DeLong (2000).

with others, feelings of self-esteem, respect for others, genuine job satisfaction, and personal growth.

The pursuit of our interests, especially material needs (including health), requires both the rule of law and private property rights. Both were basically nonexistent in the centuries of stagnant economic growth, as seen in Figure 2.1. These remain key issues today. Figure 2.2 compares economic freedom (including measures of the strength of the rule of law and private property rights) to per-capita GDP. Given a choice, who would prefer to live in a country with severely limited freedom such as Angola or Iran versus Ireland or Australia?

The second reason that explains the low levels of wealth creation in past centuries can be found in the work of William Baumol (2008). He argues

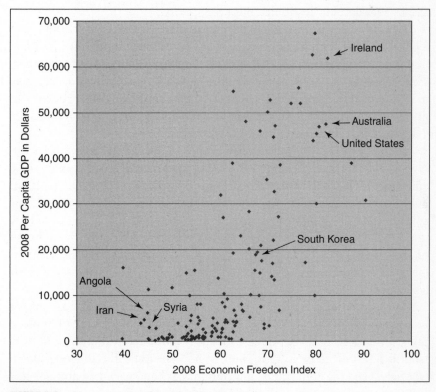

FIGURE 2.2   Economic Freedom and Wealth Creation
Source: Holmes, Feulner, and O'Grady (2008), and World Economic Outlook Database (April 2009), International Monetary Fund.

that a society's culture provides incentives (rules of the game) that motivate entrepreneurs (high-skill, high-energy, creative people) either to be productive or nonproductive. Productive entrepreneurs start and grow businesses, and turn inventions into commercial innovations, all the while improving productivity and creating value for consumers in a multitude of ways. Instead of creating wealth, nonproductive entrepreneurs "creatively" use government to redistribute wealth to the benefit of themselves and their supporters (e.g., Russia today) or engage in organized crime and corruption.

Baumol documents how his view of entrepreneurial behavior goes a long way in explaining the lack of economic progress of past centuries. Ancient Rome's technological advancements (water mill, mechanical gearing, a working steam engine, etc.) did not result in much economic benefit. Rome's society considered wealth a desirable goal as long as it was not derived from business activity, which incurred a loss in prestige. In fact, freed slaves dominated Roman business activity.

One other noteworthy example, among many described by Baumol, was medieval China with its technological advancements that did not translate into economic progress. In that period, the imperial government routinely confiscated the property of the wealthy and this was clearly a disincentive to create visible commercial activity. As for incentive, high prestige and powerful government positions were awarded to those who could pass the extraordinarily difficult imperial examinations.

A third reason for the sustained economic growth in the centuries following the Industrial Revolution was the presence of policies, networks, and institutions that disseminated useful knowledge. Joel Mokyr (2002) points out the difference between *propositional* knowledge (scientific discoveries) and *prescriptive* knowledge (inventions and techniques as to how to do things, such as write software). His key point is that the co-evolution of these two types of knowledge paved the way for sustained advancements in the quantity, quality, and affordability of products and services for consumers.

During the nineteenth century, scientific progress led to a far deeper understanding of the physical world that fed into a wide range of applications (inventions and techniques). In turn, those applications raised new, fruitful problems to be solved. Think of how scientific discoveries in chemistry advanced the commercial innovation that complemented and directed further scientific progress, all for the benefit of consumers.

Importantly, Mokyr emphasizes that the cost of communicating that new knowledge was greatly reduced with the advancements in printing and the postal service. In addition, a worldwide community developed that was comprised of scientists and engineers who had a strong motivation to communicate with one another.

To sum up, there is a thread among the three reasons that explains the low-wealth-creation centuries as well as the sustained wealth creation of recent centuries. We began by noting the absence of the prerequisites to a functioning free-market system—that is, freedom, the rule of law, and private property rights—to explain low-wealth-creation centuries. Baumol's focus on the critical role of productive entrepreneurship certainly comes under the free-market umbrella. In addition, Mokyr's focus on feedback and communication is an integral part of a free-market system in high-wealth-creation centuries. Figure 2.3 shows the central role of a free-market culture in generating wealth.

There is a higher meta-social system that determines at what point in time, and to what extent, a society is able to support a free-market economy. This higher-order social system determines the rules of the game for economic activity—that is, institutions. In other words, institutions evolve as an expression of a society's culture, and help or hinder the functioning of the free market, and therefore, the extent of wealth creation.

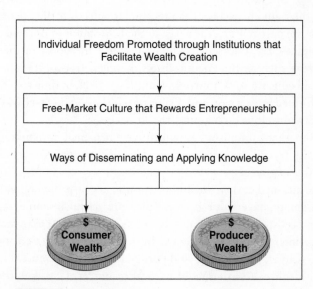

FIGURE 2.3 System Levels

Institutions provide the basic structure by which human beings throughout history have created order and attempted to reduce uncertainty in exchange. Together with the technology employed, they determine transaction and transformation costs and hence the profitability and feasibility of engaging in economic activity. They connect the past with the present and the future so that history is a largely incremental story of institutional evolution in which the historical performance of economies can only be understood as a part of a sequential story.

(North, 1990, p. 118)

Consumer wealth is the capability, over a lifetime, for consumers to acquire products and services they want. For consumers, wealth is a function of both their ability to fund purchases as well as the presence of a market of available products and services for purchase. Specifically, current consumer wealth is the sum of one's current net worth plus the value of one's human capital (job skills and work ethic) for generating future income.

Business firm, or producer, wealth reflects the ability of a firm to efficiently produce what consumers want and to create innovative products and services that generate new consumer demand. The wealth of business firms (either their public or private market value) is quantifiable as the present value of their anticipated net cash receipt streams over the life of the firm.

Over the past century, the surge in the U.S. standard of living, measured as per-capita GDP, does not adequately reflect the boost in the quality of life in areas such as therapeutic drugs, surgery, transportation, consumer goods, and education. Who would want to go back in time to when surgery was performed with a saw and a shot of whiskey, and travel was limited to horse-drawn wagons on manure-strewn streets?

Free-market capitalism has enormously benefited humankind, and that noteworthy record deserves much wider appreciation. We should want to nurture this engine of progress.

As mentioned earlier, wealth creation is about providing value to consumers. Things have value because they are useful in some way to meet consumer needs, inclusive of wants as well as necessities. At a somewhat deeper and more interesting level, as noted by Mokyr, the wealth-creation process is about creating, transmitting, and putting knowledge to practical use.

Consider wealth in terms of natural resources. Gasoline, for example, did not "exist" independent of our knowledge base. Rather, it was created through a growth in knowledge about how to combine and manipulate nature's stuff in ways that prove useful to consumers (Romer, 1994).

Knowledge accumulated over human history is embodied in the tools that economists call *capital* (Baetjer and Lewin, 2007). Knowledge-based tools are used to create wealth. For example, when you buy a drill to bore 3/8-inch holes for running wires for your new electronic gear, you buy a tool that embodies knowledge. The knowledge consists of ideas about electric motors, metallurgy, and the like that have proven useful and are part of accepted scientific knowledge. The iron ore, copper, and other metals in the drill already existed in nature; and, due to gains in knowledge, these resources were transformed into something useful to consumers. Also, keep in mind that you do not really want a drill; rather, you want 3/8-inch holes. The point is that capital is embodied knowledge in a *form that has value because it meets consumer needs*.

The surge in the standard of living beginning with the Industrial Revolution in the late eighteenth and early nineteenth centuries is the story about creating and transforming knowledge into things consumers want to buy. It took place in no small measure due to a culture that favored the dynamics of free-market capitalism, which translates into continuous commercial innovation.

Summary of Key Ideas

- On one hand, in the wake of the housing and credit crisis of 2008–2009, there was far too little recognition of the government's role in contributing to the crisis. On the other hand, investment banks and other financial institutions coupled extraordinary leverage to complex and highly risky financial instruments. The resulting short-term profits to these institutions were illusory. The faulty assessments of risk caused massive losses to the firms involved and initiated a widespread financial crisis.

- The challenge is for regulations to be designed and implemented that foster innovation that benefits consumers while ensuring the resilience of the overall financial system.

- Regulations to presumably fix perceived problems can be ineffective and produce unintended bad consequences. Effective regulatory design requires a comprehensive systems mindset that focuses on uncovering problems at an early stage similar to how high-reliability organizations

(Continued)

operate. Managements of financial institutions should be motivated (compensated) to seek sustainable, long-term profits while monitoring their operations to quickly recognize unfamiliar risks.

- A prerequisite to economic progress is freedom to take actions intended to meet consumer needs. Critical to sustained progress is for a society's institutions, or rules of behavior, to evolve in ways that promote voluntary exchange and the efficient use of resources. To sustain the public's trust in a free-market system, people need to believe that the functioning goal of the system is to efficiently provide value to consumers.

CHAPTER 3

The Ideal Free-Market System

*The fundamental threat to freedom is power to coerce, be it in
the hands of a monarch, a dictator, an oligarchy, or a momentary
majority. The preservation of freedom requires the elimination
of such concentration of power to the fullest possible extent
and the dispersal and distribution of whatever power cannot be
eliminated—a system of checks and balances. By removing the
organization of economic activity from the control of political
authority, the market eliminates this source of coercive power. It
enables economic strength to be a check to political power rather
than a reinforcement.*

— Milton Friedman, *Capitalism and Freedom*

In Chapter 2 we noted that, for a free-market system to function, a society
must promote freedom for people to broadly pursue their interests, protect
private property rights, and enforce the rule of law that protects the life and
liberty of everyone regardless of their wealth or status. As institutions evolve
to advance these goals, a free-market system can then prosper. For example,
the development of the limited-liability corporation, and of markets for trading stocks and bonds, were enormously important to capital formation and
to the free-market process for allocating resources to their best uses.

The free-market system is built on matching success or failure in serving
customers with rewards or losses. Government actions, by way of bailouts
or protective tariffs, interfere with that reward system and lead to an inefficient allocation of resources. Firms that are woefully short of the skills necessary for providing value to customers at competitive prices need to greatly

improve; or they should go bankrupt so their resources and employees can be shifted to more productive activities.

COMPONENTS OF A FREE-MARKET SYSTEM

Let's analyze what a free-market system is and how it delivers value to consumers.[1] We can begin at the lower-left box of Figure 3.1.

Economic progress starts with, and grows from, a society's *capital base*. Capital is embodied knowledge of what has been learned in the past that is useful for producing what consumers want in the future. Capital can be classified as tangible (buildings, machines, roads, etc.) or intangible (codified knowledge, tacit skills [Leonard and Swap, 2004], and methods used for acquiring new knowledge).

Voluntary exchange occurs when people willingly exchange goods and services with others to improve their condition. When exchanges are voluntary, both parties benefit, giving up something they value less in order to gain something they value more. Exchanges can be by barter or by money, immediate (retail sales) or involve commitments over time (insurance, investments). Voluntary exchange is a prerequisite for sustained wealth creation.

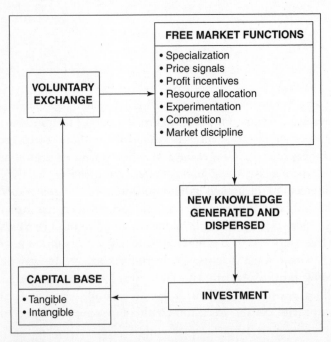

FIGURE 3.1   Free-Market System Focused on Consumers

Voluntary exchange creates opportunities for *specialization*. That is, individuals specialize in producing goods and services at a "low" cost due to their skill and efficiency. They trade those for desired goods and services that would be "high" cost for them to produce. The more capital a society has and the more opportunities for voluntary exchange that exist (the breadth and depth of markets), the more specialization can take place. People can avoid being hunters and farmers out of necessity, and instead can pursue work that offers the best opportunities for generating income and job satisfaction. Combining one's specialized labor with capital increases productivity, that is, creates greater useful output for the same hours worked.

Market pricing is essential for both parties to benefit from voluntary exchange. Prices communicate information. *Price signals* coordinate action by providing *profit incentives* to effectively allocate and use resources (Hayek, 1945). Business enterprises respond to the profit incentive and act with the expectation of earning economic profit by efficiently providing products and services in amounts that "the market" wants. Over the long term, the bigger the gain in profits, the more value-added has been delivered to customers. Price controls, rent controls, and a variety of government subsidies distort the market's price signals and lead to inefficiencies for the many, while transferring wealth to a favored few.

Profit incentives drive *resource allocation* as firms adjust to current market prices and expectations of future prices. Based on their existing knowledge, it is not always obvious to firms' top decision makers how to best use resources or how to develop new, innovative ways to better meet customer needs. That often entails *experimentation*, which necessarily implies failure as well as success. Markets facilitate the discovery of new ways to serve customers. Experimentation is as critical to sustained economic progress as it is to the growth of knowledge in the physical sciences. The success (or failure) of business experiments can be judged by their effect on firms' profits.

Firms continually aim to surpass competitors, better serve customers, and earn additional profits. If they fail to exploit new ideas, technology, or the myriad ways of improving processes, their efficiency declines compared to the competition. Then they lose customers, which results in lower profits or actual losses. As the following quote brings to life, the status quo is never a long-term, viable option:

My central contention here is that what differentiates the prototype capitalist economy most sharply from all other economic systems is free-market pressures that force firms into a continuing process of innovation, *because it becomes a matter of life and death for many of them.* The static efficiency properties that are stressed by standard welfare economics are emphatically not the most important qualities of capitalist economies. Rather, what is clear to historians and laypersons alike is that capitalism is unique in the extraordinary growth record it has been able to achieve; in its recurring industrial revolutions that have produced an outpouring of material wealth unlike anything previously seen in human history.

Moreover, it seems indisputable that innovation accounts for much of this enviable growth record. But what attributes of capitalism are responsible for this dramatic superiority in its record of innovation? The answer I propose here is that in key parts of the economy the prime weapon of competition is not price but innovation . . . . The result is a ferocious arms race among the firms in the most rapidly evolving sectors of the economy, with innovation as the prime weapon.

(Baumol, 2002, pp. viii–ix, italics in the original)

The hallmark of a free market is *competition* among business firms. Customers benefit through lower prices than otherwise would prevail and in particular, as noted by William Baumol in the above quote, through continuous innovation that leads to improved products and services.

How does competition weed out inefficient firms? The stock market is an especially illuminating lens by which to observe *market discipline.* If a firm steadfastly fails to earn the opportunity cost of capital, its stock price suffers. Then, there is pressure to hire new management, which often jettisons old business strategies, downsizes, fires employees, and refocuses the firm's resources. At times, failing businesses (especially small firms) can quickly go bankrupt. Less apparent to the general public is that the harsh punishment administered by the market creates new job opportunities as resources flow to other firms that are better skilled at efficiently providing value.

Although wealth is created by this constant cycling of resources from less-efficient to more-efficient firms, this process is invisible to the general public. In contrast, the negatives are narrowly focused and highly visible to the public (closed operations, workers fired, communities harmed). The public's perception tends to be heavily influenced by general media reports that myopically sensationalize the negative cost of adapting to change (e.g., outsourcing) and totally ignore the long-term benefits.

Voluntary exchange, specialization, price signals, profits, and competition all generate and help disperse *new knowledge* about consumer wants, the best ways to meet those wants, and investment opportunities. In a competitive free market, there is not only continual innovation and the generation of new knowledge, but also a rapid and widespread dissemination and practical application of that knowledge as firms, investors, and consumers respond to it. Markets, which on their surface seem to be about material goods, are actually mostly about ideas and knowledge.

New knowledge created by market processes encourages, directs, and rewards new *investment* in the creation of and delivery of goods and services. New investment flows into the capital base, which then accelerates mutually beneficial voluntary exchanges and sets off another round of the wealth-creation cycle.

Consider, for a moment, the absence of one or more of the basic prerequisites to a free-market system, and consider how much investment there would be: in a lawless society?; in one that fails to provide for and protect an individual's property rights?; if the corporate form of business organization did not exist?; if there were no existing market mechanism for readily buying and selling stocks and bonds? With an effectively functioning free market, investments offer the opportunity for financial rewards while automatically increasing the capital base, and sowing the seeds for future increases in productivity and in the standard of living.

CONSUMER WEALTH, PRODUCER WEALTH, AND COMPETITION

One obvious and common way to assess consumer wealth is to visit a country and observe the living conditions there. Alternatively, a more quantitative way is to tabulate people's net worth and estimate the value of their human capital (knowledge and skills). But to understand the process of how wealth is created, one needs to analyze how firms enable consumers to buy more of what they want at a lower price (e.g., computing power) and to receive higher-quality goods and services (automobile travel compared to traveling on horses). Figure 3.2 shows the connection between consumer wealth and producer wealth.

The back-and-forth arrow in Figure 3.2 connects Consumer Wealth and Producer Wealth. This is because employees working at firms receive paychecks, and at the same time are consumers. Moreover, their consumer wealth is partly comprised of stock and debt ownership of firms through 401(k)s

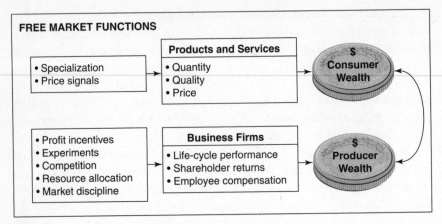

FIGURE 3.2 Consumer Wealth and Producer Wealth

and other forms of saving and investing. The arrow is also a reminder of the cause-and-effect complexity of a global system of wealth creation.

As to a global economy, how often have we heard politicians say that we must get better at competing for jobs in the global marketplace, and here is the plan for doing so? And that plan entails all sorts of imposed distortions to the market system that either interfere with voluntary exchange, or grant some sort of anticompetitive advantage to businesses with political clout.

A plausible case can be made that the "competition for jobs" issue is better analyzed as "competition for capital" (Rutledge, 2008). High corporate tax rates lower firms' after-tax returns on capital. The United States has one of the highest corporate tax rates among the more developed countries. Making matters worse, the complexity of the corporate tax code is mindboggling. It is an open invitation for unproductive entrepreneurial activity and massive lobbying that distorts the free-market system. The return to investors gets reduced even further by taxes on interest, dividends, and capital gains.

In an interconnected global economy, all else equal, capital seeks out the highest expected returns, net of all taxes. When financial capital flows into a particular country to fund business expansion, employees in that country get better tools and knowhow to become more productive. Increased productivity is the key to higher wages and expanded employment opportunities. The CEO of FedEx, which has 290,000 employees, has noted that about 70 percent of the return from their capital expenditures in equipment, planes, computer systems and the like is realized by employees in the form of higher wages as their productivity rises (Moore, 2008).

EFFICIENTLY PROVIDING WHAT CONSUMERS WANT

Understanding the wealth-creation process has implications for government policymakers, business leaders, and investors. The message put in the briefest way is: Give top priority to consumers. The best way to accomplish this is through a free-market system that has a high degree of competition with a minimum of government interference that distorts the competitive playing field.

Particularly insightful empirical work on comparisons of wealth creation across countries is summarized in *The Power of Productivity* by William W. Lewis (2004). He headed up a large-scale, 12-year study by the McKinsey Global Institute that analyzed industry productivity across 13 countries. The data from this unique, bottom-up, field research revealed the critical importance of competition to economic performance.

This research pointed out that zoning laws, exclusion of foreign competition, government subsidies, tax burdens that promote an underground (informal) economy to the detriment of legitimate companies, and assorted government favors to special interests all work to preserve inefficiency with higher prices and lower quality for consumers. Inefficient firms continue their wasteful ways because the rules of the game minimize competition from efficient firms.

For example, small retailers in Japan have been protected through zoning laws and government subsidies. This contrasts with the extremely efficient Japanese industries that compete globally (e.g., autos, electronics). Small Japanese retailers are quite inefficient. In the United States, in contrast, Wal-Mart has spurred productivity increases throughout the retail industry, including its suppliers. Brazil has an exceedingly large underground economy that pays no taxes and is also quite inefficient. But the much more efficient Brazilian companies in the formal sector are hit with a heavy tax burden. This interferes with the competitive process and makes it difficult for the tax-paying formal sector to take market share away from the tax-free, informal sector.

The short-term impact of increased competition would cause problems for inefficient firms and their employees, but would improve the standard of living for consumers in general. After an adjustment period, employees would be better off as firms adapt and resources shift to more skilled firms.

The absence of a systems mindset can easily result in shortsighted thinking, and lead to bad decisions. Interfering with competition to keep wages high and employment temporarily up at inefficient firms may appear to help employees; but that comes at a high cost to others and, in the long run, is not sustainable.

Recall that one of the bullet points under the "Actions and Consequences" component of the PAK Loop in Chapter 1 states that cause and effect have both time and spatial lags. This is at the heart of the dilemma in which people benefit enormously from free-market capitalism; but the needed allocation adjustments can temporarily result in an unstable and insecure environment for those affected. On the surface, the system appears not to be working to many hardworking and capable people who have been fired.

To avoid excessive regulations and gain widespread support for free-market capitalism, we need sustained and robust economic growth that reduces the political incentive to "fix" the economy with programs that distort the basic function of consumer choice and competition. In this regard, two private-sector proposals, discussed in later chapters, merit consideration.

The first proposal is to accelerate implementation of lean management geared toward providing high value to customers while continually purging waste. This is often talked about by CEOs and boards of directors, but companies rarely achieve, on a sustained basis, anywhere near the extraordinary productivity of Toyota, whose Toyota Production System pioneered lean principles.

A particularly important part of lean management is the continual mentoring of employees to improve their *problem-solving skills*. As lean firms adapt to new business opportunities, employees are better equipped to transition to different jobs due to highly developed, general-purpose problem-solving skills that are integral to a lean business culture. Chapter 6 reviews lean principles and the issues involved when companies decide to make a lean transformation.

The second proposal addresses the situation in which insufficiently skilled CEOs are retained for many years by underperforming boards of directors. Often, these boards are comprised of directors whose membership on the board is due to their personal relationship with the CEO.

The public, in general, and shareholders in particular, are rightfully angered by the enormous compensation, including golden parachutes, received by underperforming CEOs upon termination (Bebchuk and Fried, 2004). At the level of the firm, stability and employment security could be greatly improved by a process that upgrades the quality of board oversight so that boards effectively monitor the development of a lean culture attuned to long-term wealth creation and led by highly skilled CEOs.

Ineffective board oversight is manifested by CEOs who run inefficient operations typically with a "grow-the-business" mindset that is disconnected from economic efficiency and wealth-creation principles. Chapter 7 describes a market-based approach for improving corporate governance. Importantly, the proposed solution avoids heavy-handed government intervention that could easily produce unintended bad consequences. The reasoning behind this initiative is rooted in a sound understanding of how wealth is created. The starting point is the firms' competitive life cycle, which is explained in detail and illustrated with company examples in the next chapter.

Summary of Key Ideas

- Critics of free-market capitalism tend to lack an understanding of the synergistic operation of the components of a free-market system (Figure 3.1). Critics assert that they occupy the moral high ground because of their opposition to greed and excessive profits. That this assertion is false is demonstrated by the significantly higher levels of per-capita income, life expectancy, education, and democracy for those societies that more closely embrace free-market principles.

- Business firms are the key to a free-market system that benefits consumers through efficiency and innovation in delivering products and services. A deeper understanding of the economy from a bottom-up perspective of business firms by public policymakers (and the voters who elect them) should lead to legislation and regulations that are decidedly more pro–wealth creation.

- Knowledge growth and wealth creation are opposite sides of the same coin. In a competitive, free-market system, innovation, as noted by William Baumol, becomes a matter of life and death for many firms. Managements of firms that gain competitive advantage typically have orchestrated fast and effective learning throughout their organizations so that innovation becomes part of the firm's culture.

- In a global economy, competition is clearly seen as intense for products and services. Not nearly as visible is the competition for capital, in which investors seek the highest expected returns adjusted for taxes and risk. Tax rates on businesses and investors are crucial determinants of the return on capital. This impacts the amount of new investments made, which affects productivity and job growth.

CHAPTER 4

The Competitive Life-Cycle View of the Firm

There is no more important proposition in economic theory than that, under competition, the rate of return on investment tends towards equality in all industries. Entrepreneurs will seek to leave relatively unprofitable industries and enter relatively profitable industries.

—George Stigler, *Capital and Rates of Return in Manufacturing Industries*

Discussions about wealth creation and economic growth tend to involve aggregate measures of GDP, productivity, and the like, but the real action takes place at the firm level.[1] Over time, firms' publicly traded stocks and bonds let us more directly measure producer wealth (equity and debt), which can be connected to its root cause, namely firms' long-term financial performance. This connection, which can be established using what I call the *competitive life-cycle framework*, provides uniquely valuable microeconomic data to policymakers, business leaders, and investors.

COMPETITIVE LIFE-CYCLE FRAMEWORK

The following eight points begin to explain how the competitive life-cycle framework connects firms' financial performance to stock prices:

1. The *goal* of the firm should be to efficiently serve existing customer needs and to efficiently commercialize innovative new products and services

that will be in demand in the future. This does not mean efficiency in an accounting sense, such as the cost of a unit produced. Excess production at a lower average cost per unit does not represent a gain in efficiency. Rather, efficiency improves as less resources are used to produce and better deliver precisely what customers want, when they want it, and without any of the hassles that waste consumers' time and money (Womack and Jones, 2005). Successful management of a firm results in value delivered to customers over the long term with benefits accruing to both employees and shareholders.

2. *Managerial skill* is reflected in the vitality of the firm's culture and the usefulness of the firm's knowledge base so that existing processes keep improving and changes in the external environment are turned into future opportunities.

3. Firms face a *competitive life cycle* during which managerial skill continually confronts the force of competition. In economic terms, the bottom line of the competitive struggle is the firm's long-term, expected net cash receipt stream—the primary determinant of producer wealth.

4. The *life-cycle valuation model* helps one to forecast and value net cash receipts in an intuitive manner, keyed to managerial skill and competition.

5. At any point in a firm's life cycle, management's *resource allocation decisions* should be focused on transitioning to a new life-cycle position that is favorable vis-à-vis competitive pressures.

6. Risk-adjusted, *total shareholder returns* for a particular time period will be greater (less) than the market return if the ending life-cycle position is more (less) favorable than investor expectations at the beginning of the period.

7. Bubbles in the stock market lead to expectations of firms' future financial performance that are hard to justify on economic grounds. Nevertheless, on average, and over longer time periods, investor expectations turn out to be astute forecasts of the future. Consequently, management can obtain a *reality check* regarding their strategy and skillfulness in execution by quantifying, at any point in time, a snapshot of investor expectations. This exercise reveals a firm's expected future life-cycle pattern of economic returns and reinvestment rates, and can be compared to similarly calculated expectations for industry competitors.

8. The competitive life-cycle framework provides insights into the historical record of wealth creation for any particular firm. It ties the results of key managerial activities to a time series of economic returns, reinvestment rates, and investor discount rates (i.e., required returns) that explain the firm's wealth creation or dissipation. The competitive

life-cycle view illuminates *economic reasons for the levels and changes in any specific firm's stock prices over the long term.*

These eight points suggest that insightful business histories, that is, *long-term track records of key performance variables*, are necessary guideposts for managements, boards of directors, and investors. The components of such track record displays help promote a dialogue between firms and the capital markets that is presently missing. Such a wealth-creation dialogue is necessary as an antidote to the current *simplistic* dialogue, which is focused on a single accounting earnings number. A more useful dialogue would address the *complex* managerial tasks involved with both achieving satisfactory near-term operating cash flows and securing long-term competitive advantage.

Specifying the components of a track record that are useful for explaining firms' market valuations is straightforward. In Chapter 5, a warranted value, at any point in time, using discounted cash flow, is defined as the present value of an anticipated *net cash receipt (NCR)* stream using a firm's cost of capital as the discount rate. Think of NCRs as operating cash inflows into a firm, less required cash outflows for any new investment that is needed. I realize that the previous sentences may have elicited a groan from readers who are unfamiliar with financial jargon. Please do not despair. Chapter 5, which deals with finance details, can be skipped as it is not essential to understanding the other chapters.

Consider a bond whose NCRs are interest and principal payments. The current market value of the bond is the present value of these NCRs discounted at a rate that equals the yield-to-maturity. With stocks, the same discounted cash flow principles apply, but the NCRs are a bit more challenging to estimate.

The most important variable that determines a firm's NCRs is its economic returns. When a firm invests in a project, such as an oil well, the economic result is reflected in cash outflows and cash inflows over the useful life of the well. The return-on-investment (ROI) based on cash flows over the life of the well is the economic return.

FIRMS' COMPETITIVE LIFE CYCLES AND DYNAMISM

Figure 4.1 is a graphic representation of a firm's stylized history, showing transitions through different life-cycle stages. At any point in time, a firm's market value depends on investor expectations for the four variables in this figure.

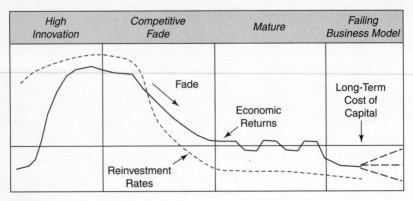

FIGURE 4.1 Firms' Competitive Life Cycle
Source: Madden (2005a).

In the life-cycle framework one can observe the effects of Joseph Schumpeter's creative destruction at work:

> ... [the] kind of competition which counts ... competition from the new commodity, the new technology, the new source of supply, the new type of organizations ... competition which commands a decisive cost or quality advantage and which strikes not at the margins of the profits and the outputs of the existing firms but at their foundations and their very lives.
>
> (Schumpeter, 1950, p. 84)

Frequently, the radical competition that Schumpeter alludes to comes from the *high innovation*–stage firms. These firms have successfully developed a business that meets the fundamental criterion of wealth creation, namely *economic returns* (cash-based ROIs) well in excess of the *cost of capital*. Particularly successful firms exhibit high *reinvestment rates* in response to a high demand for their products or services, and this creates additional wealth.

Next, firms enter the *competitive fade* stage (Wiggins and Ruefli, 2005). Attracted by sizable wealth-creation opportunities, competitors attempt to duplicate, and improve on, the innovative product/service. Due to competitive pressure, firms' economic returns *fade* toward the cost of capital, and reinvestment rates *fade* to lower levels (Fama and French, 2000). Optimizing wealth creation at any stage of a life cycle revolves around critical decisions that have the potential to produce more favorable long-term fade rates.

Then, a firm enters the *mature* life-cycle stage. Due to past successes, management typically is lulled into a business-as-usual complacency at the very time when top priority should be given to elevating economic returns.

Finally, a lack of innovation, coupled to companywide bureaucratic inefficiencies, usually accompanies a transition to the *failing business model* stage. At this stage, purging business-as-usual practices or downsizing are invariably required if the firm is to recover and avoid bankruptcy.

The notion of competition driving above-average profitability down toward the average, or cost of capital level, is not an abstract argument. It has been an observed phenomenon for a long time. In his *Principles of Political Economy* (a popular economics textbook of the mid-1800s), John Stuart Mill describes how capital moves in response to "expectations of profit" such that "a sort of balance is restored" (Mill, 2004, p. 393). The point is that skill and competition are timeless principles that ultimately determine long-term profitability.

While Schumpeter's view of the entrepreneur is relevant and highly engaging, it is a bit simplistic. Edmund Phelps stresses the concept of *economic dynamism*, which refers to an economy's degree of success in commercializing innovations:

Dynamism—or the lack of it—tends to manifest itself in a variety of ways. Higher dynamism in an economy delivers faster productivity growth most, if not all, of the time so with time it leads to a consistently higher *level* of productivity. Dynamism creates a distinctive sector of economic activity: employment in the financing, development and marketing of new commercial products for launch into the marketplace; and a cadre of managers deciding what to produce and how to produce it. These added avenues of employment, it may be argued, generate higher levels of total labor force and total employment. There is also evidence that higher dynamism results in workers reporting higher job satisfaction and employee engagement. Finally, higher dynamism also tends to produce a relatively high rate of "turnover" in the members belonging to the economy's largest firms, as some new firms grow large and displace old members.

(Phelps, 2008, p. 2, italics in original)

Phelps's dynamism suggests that sustained economic progress involves much more than the intermittent big advancement (e.g., scientific break-through) lauded by Schumpeter. Sustained progress requires institutions and attitudes that support wealth creation as previously depicted in Figure 2.3. Compatible with this view, Amar Bhidé (2008) makes the case that a nation's capacity to exploit cutting-edge research, *regardless of where the R&D occurred*, is the key to economic competitiveness.

The more we view economic progress from a systems mindset perspective, the more evident the importance of diversity and innovation. Stuart Kaufman stresses the importance of diversity, that is, the potential to spawn innovative complements and substitutes for existing goods and services. For example, the arrival of television led to the remote-control TV channel changer (a complement).

It is hard to imagine more fertile soil for diversity and innovation than a functioning free market, based on economic freedom, coupled to institutions and cultural attitudes that help translate big advancements such as the automobile into a stream of successful commercial innovations.

> When the car was invented, it created the conditions for the oil industry, the gas industry, paved roads, traffic lights, traffic police, bribing traffic police, motels, car washes, fast-food restaurants, and suburbia in what is called a Schumpeterian gale of creative destruction. The destructive side of the story is the extinction of the horse, buggy, saddlery, smithy, and pony express in the United States, as widely used technologies. *The creative parts of the Schumpeterian gale, gas, motels, and suburbia, etc. are all complements to the car. Together they make a kind of autocatalytic, mutually sustaining economic-technological ecosystem of complements that commandeer economic capital resources into that autocatalytic web and can create vast wealth.* All these ways of making a living are largely mutually necessary for one another and they have coevolved together for about a century. Conversely, the hula hoop seems to have few complements or substitutes. It can enter or leave the economic web without creating an avalanche loss of old ways of making a living, or creating new ways of making a living.
>
> (Kaufman, 2008, pp. 159–160, italics in original)

In the next section, we review how well or poorly specific companies have performed over long periods of time in the United States, where conditions, by and large, were supportive of wealth creation. This also provides a bird's-eye view of turnover in which innovative firms displace the big, mature, business-as-usual firms.

COMPANY EXAMPLES

The company examples that follow were chosen because they are easy-to-understand business stories illustrating important wealth-creation and -dissipation lessons. The better one understands the past, the more equipped one is to deal with the future. Life-cycle track records help us understand how the key variables of Figure 4.1 determine long-term levels and changes in stock prices. In order to have a deeper understanding of these company histories, a brief overview of each company is included that addresses issues such as key management decisions in the past, firm culture, and the problems posed by free-market competition.

The examples begin with Eastman Kodak's life-cycle history. It clearly shows the results of the relentless pressure of competition, and a need to successfully innovate. Kodak's history reminds one that innovation is, as Baumol noted, "a matter of life and death."

The histories of IBM, Digital Equipment, and Apple Computer contain a variety of lessons about competition from the computer/information technology industry. The same lessons for the steel industry come from Bethlehem Steel and Nucor. Kmart's track record reveals a now mostly forgotten time period in its history when innovation propelled stellar stock price performance. Long-term, superior managerial skills are illustrated in the life-cycle histories of Medtronic and Donaldson. Walgreen's life cycle illustrates the challenges of evolving a business model that has been successful in the past, but faces increasingly tough competition.

The life-cycle charts in this section have three panels each. The top panel displays inflation-adjusted (real) economic returns that are estimated as a cash-flow-return-on-investment, or CFROI® metric (registered trademark of Credit Suisse Securities). The top panel includes a benchmark, long-term corporate average CFROI return of 6 percent real to approximate the cost of capital.[2] As a proxy for the firm's economic return, the CFROI metric is constructed from annual financial statements in order to approximate the average, real ROIs being achieved from the firm's portfolio of ongoing business projects. Real numbers remove distortions due to inflation (or deflation), thereby showing more accurate levels and trends in time series data.

The middle panel shows real asset growth rates that indicate the pace of reinvestment. The bottom panel is a cumulative index. It reflects annual changes in the yearly excess (positive or negative) of the total shareholder return (dividends plus price change) on the company's stock relative to the S&P 500. A positive share performance versus the S&P 500 is depicted by rising trends in the relative wealth index, performance matching the market is displayed as flat trends, and negative performance by falling trends.

When analyzing a life-cycle figure, keep in mind that the long-term fade patterns for economic returns and reinvestment rates are often influenced for a period of years by favorable/unfavorable economic shocks. But, the primary long-term determinant of fade is managerial skill—especially skill in crafting and adapting a viable business model for each of the firm's major businesses. For established firms, the hallmark of an underperforming business model is reflected in an average level of CFROI returns below the required cost of capital. In contrast, sustained levels of CFROI returns above the cost of capital, especially when coupled with significant reinvestment rates, indicate high managerial skill.

A business model is a system with four major components (Johnson, Christensen, and Kagermann, 2008):

1. A customer value proposition.
2. Targets for financial variables to create value for both customers and shareholders.
3. Key resources.
4. Key processes.

A common situation is one in which management was successful in executing a particular business model in the past, so their perception of the world became dominated by the assumption that what worked well in the past will continue to do so. The knowledge-building process, encapsulated by the PAK Loop, then becomes stymied due to a lost opportunity for feedback to show the limitations of existing knowledge.

Early recognition of upcoming competitive shortfalls provides time needed to experiment without being under the crush of serious cash flow problems. Late recognition invariably results in the eventual need for a large-scale purging of business as usual and attendant employee dismissals. The key to early adaptation by top management is to actively seek feedback that can:

- Reveal weaknesses in strongly held assumptions about existing business models.
- Identify the root causes of waste.
- Generate insights for exploring new opportunities through appropriate business models.

In short, management needs to nurture fast and effective PAK Loops. Skilled managements make every day a learning day for themselves and their employees.

Eastman Kodak

In 1888, George Eastman began selling the Kodak camera and the film for it, which made photography available to the general public. His customer value proposition was strikingly effective, "You press the button, we do the rest."

During the 1960s, Kodak introduced its Instamatic camera, which had a film cartridge instead of a film roll. The success of the Instamatic resulted in CFROI returns surging in the mid-1960s to substantially above the long-term, 6 percent cost-of-capital benchmark, as shown in the upper panel of Figure 4.2.[3] CFROI returns held at a wealth-creating level of about 12 percent until the mid-1970s. Investors were surprised by this performance, and Kodak outperformed the market (lower panel) during this time.

But since the mid-1970s, Kodak has substantially underperformed the market. The gut issue has been a failure to successfully adapt its business model to the new world of fast-changing technology. In 1994, *Fortune* magazine noted that, regardless of its endless restructurings, Kodak remained "one of the most bureaucratic, wasteful, paternalistic, slow-moving, isolated, and beloved companies in America" (Nulty, 1994).

Kodak's culture was rooted in an obsession with quality, to the detriment of any concern with the time it takes to develop new products. This was coupled with extraordinary vertical integration to achieve ever more control. These factors contributed to Kodak's decline in profitability during the past three decades.

Kodak's foray into instant photography was totally mismanaged, which resulted in failure as well as a $900 million payment to Polaroid for patent infringement. Over the years, management's lack of a viable business model became evident in their grab-bag of acquisitions. Typical of those years

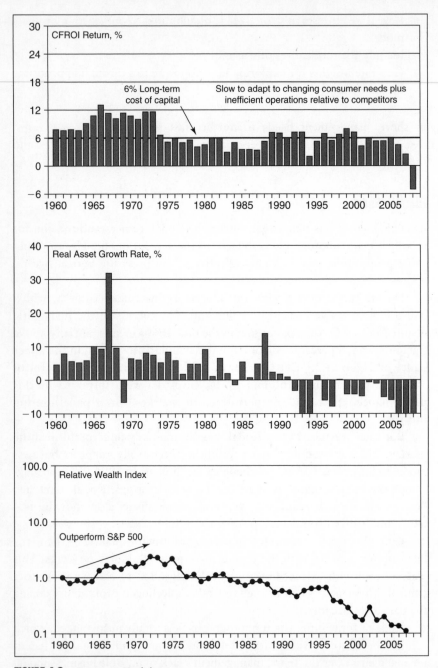

FIGURE 4.2 Eastman Kodak
Source: Credit Suisse HOLT ValueSearch® global database.

was the lack of strategic vision for the high-priced acquisition of Sterling Drug—which was later divested. Apparently, the board of directors viewed its top priority as supporting management's decisions. In 1984, 8 directors out of a total of 15 were insiders.

Further, the company was slow to adapt to digital photography and was significantly hurt in the film arena by competition from Fuji. Eventually, Kodak made substantial innovations in digital photography, but then failed on the second component of a business model, profits. Its profits were meager even though the quality delivered to customers was high.

What impresses me in studying the details of Kodak's numerous acquisitions, divestitures, and restructurings is the lack of managerial skill. Earlier in this chapter, it was pointed out that "managerial skill is reflected in the vitality of the firm's culture and the usefulness of the firm's *knowledge base* so existing processes keep improving and changes in the external environment are turned into future opportunities." By any measure, the speed of improving Kodak's organizational knowledge base has been pathetically slow.

In a 2006 *Business Week* article, Kodak's new CEO, Antonio Perez, remarked on the firm's hierarchical culture, which clearly believes in the omnipotence of leadership: "If I said it was raining, nobody would argue with me, even if it was sunny outside" (Hamm and Symonds, 2006). Perez seems to be addressing the root causes of Kodak's long-term decline. Today, the challenges are huge and the competition formidable.

IBM

In Chapter 1, perceptions of the external world were shown to be heavily influenced by one's knowledge base, in particular, strongly held assumptions based on past experience. IBM management experienced an incredible, long-lived success with their System 360 line of computers. That bred widespread complacency among management. And that dulled their perceptual lens when they observed the competitive environment.

Above-average CFROI returns peaked in the early 1980s; and during the next 10 years, CFROI returns plummeted as personal computers radically changed the business landscape. IBM was late in recognizing that PCs would gain widespread business use. Due to difficulties working across business units, IBM outsourced the PC's most profitable components, the microprocessor to Intel and the operating system to Microsoft.

When Lou Gerstner was made CEO in 1993, IBM was hemorrhaging cash. Revenues from mainframe computers had fallen off a cliff, and IBM's other businesses were tied to mainframe sales. As for the formidable problem of the cultural beliefs that permeated the organization and sheltered obsolete assumptions, Gerstner noted:

> When there's little competitive threat, when high profit margins and a commanding market position are assumed, then the economic and market forces that other companies have to live or die by simply don't apply. In that environment, what would you expect to happen? The company and its people lose touch with external realities, because what's happening in the marketplace is essentially irrelevant to the success of the company.
>
> . . . This hermetically sealed quality—an institutional viewpoint that anything important started inside the company—was, I believe, the root cause of many of our problems . . . [leading to] a general disinterest in customer needs, accompanied by a preoccupation with internal politics. There was a general permission to stop projects dead in their tracks, a bureaucratic infrastructure that defended turf instead of promoting collaboration, and a management class that presided rather than acted. IBM even had a language all its own.
>
> (Gerstner, 2002, pp. 117, 189)

Gerstner delivered a truly remarkable restructuring of a very large company in seriously bad shape. He orchestrated a new customer value proposition that was the nucleus for the subsequent surge in CFROI returns. Mainframe computers were quickly developed with CMOS technology to deliver extraordinary value to customers. The new focus was on networked solutions that integrated technology into a firm's processes. This led to a major push into services, including software development. IBM Global Services grew revenues from $7 billion in 1992 to $30 billion in 2001. These new initiatives involved the sale of knowledge and required a new business model.

As Gerstner's restructuring changes took hold, CFROI returns shot well above the cost of capital and led to IBM's stock handily outperforming the market for many years. Sam Palmisano became CEO in 2002, and he continues to refine IBM's business model. (See Figure 4.3.)

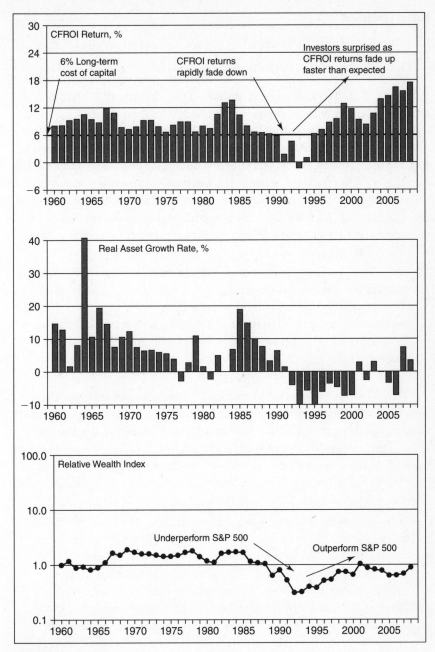

FIGURE 4.3 IBM
Source: Credit Suisse HOLT ValueSearch® global database.

Digital Equipment

Ken Olsen co-founded Digital Equipment Corporation (DEC) in 1957. Under his CEO leadership, DEC grew to $11 billion in sales in 1988 and became the thirteenth most profitable company among the Fortune 500 in that year. But during the next decade, DEC fell apart. Olsen resigned in 1992. The firm was eventually acquired by Compaq in 1998.

The business press pointed out that DEC had been wedded to minicomputers and missed the PC revolution, that it stayed with proprietary architecture too long, and that it lacked strategic direction. The far more interesting question is, Why? Edward Schein, who has done pioneering research on culture and organizations, addressed that question in his insightful 2003 book, *DEC Is Dead, Long Live DEC*. Schein had worked with DEC's Ken Olsen as a consultant for 30 years. Schein made two especially important points:

1. DEC had an unusually strong culture that was actively practiced throughout the organization.
2. Those strongly held organizational beliefs were ideal for the high-innovation, high-growth stage of DEC's life cycle, but were hugely counterproductive as DEC became a very large company and the environment changed.

DEC's culture personified Ken Olsen's beliefs: freedom from bureaucratic controls, individual responsibility, defend/sell your ideas to peers (truth-through-conflict), and a fanatical allegiance to engineering quality and elegance. DEC became a magnet as the place to work if you were a top engineer. In terms of the deep pull of cultural beliefs, Schein noted the following:

> The lessons to be learned here are about how culture works at different stages in an organization's life cycle. The very same processes can have very different outcomes at different times in the life of an organization. Culture is a complex force field that influences all of an organization's processes. *We try to manage culture but, in fact, culture manages us far more than we ever manage it, and this happens largely outside our awareness.* The most dangerous error in the analysis of culture is to overlook its tremendous yet invisible coercive qualities and its extraordinary stability. . . . What DEC learned in its growth phase is that a climate of innovation will guarantee success. This early success so strongly reinforced the DEC cultural

paradigm, and continued positive feedback from established customers was so steady, that one could see already in the late 1960s and early 1970s that DEC managers and employees were hooked. This was clearly the way to run a company.

(Schein, 2003, pp. 11, 86, italics added)

What was healthy internal competition for product ideas in the early successful years became in the later years, when DEC was a very large organization, internal warfare over resource allocation. Business opportunities were spurned if they did not conform to DEC's engineering quality and elegance standards. DEC clearly had the resources to exploit the Internet, but lacked the managerial skill to develop and implement a radically different business model in the new environment. (See Figure 4.4.)

Apple

Apple's introduction of its personal computer in the late 1970s was certainly innovative, but was it a successful commercial innovation? The answer is yes, because Apple's CFROI returns (upper panel of Figure 4.5) substantially exceeded the cost of capital in its early years as a public company. The creation of a new industry provides the early entrant with sizable opportunities to reinvest (high asset growth rates, middle panel).

But competitors are attracted to these wealth-creating opportunities. Unless firms have unique competitive advantages that are difficult to duplicate, competitors will quickly drive above-average CFROI returns downward (fast fade). This classic story of competition is played out in Apple's track record that shows CFROI returns plummeting during the 1990s.

With the introduction of the Macintosh computer in 1984, customers were ecstatic about the intuitive user experience enabled by the Mac's unique operating system. Delivered on a silver platter was the opportunity to license the Mac operating system to other PC manufacturers and become the industry standard. Apple passed on this licensing opportunity, and Microsoft's Windows eventually won the enormously profitable prize of being the industry standard. What kind of thinking led to that decision?

The problem was top management's mindset that was riveted to a business model that constrained Apple to be a hardware company (Linzmayer, 2004, p. 249). They myopically perceived licensing as a diversion, which would hurt Mac sales. They needed to think more like a software company, where big profits come from providing the software that everyone uses.

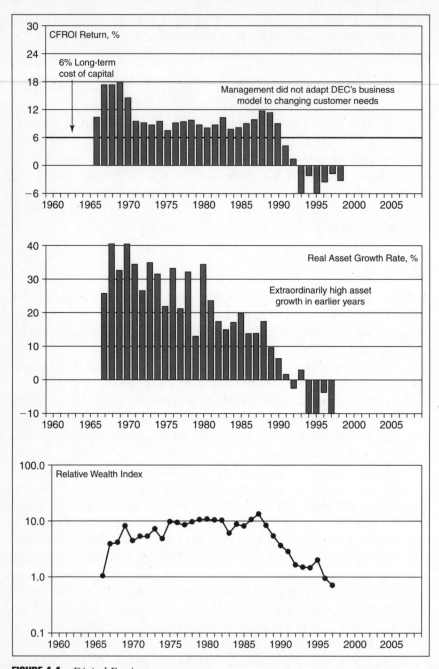

FIGURE 4.4   Digital Equipment
Source: Credit Suisse HOLT ValueSearch® global database.

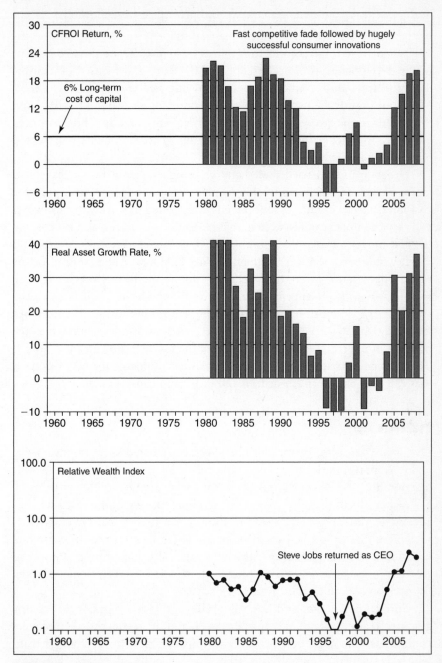

FIGURE 4.5   Apple
Source: Credit Suisse HOLT ValueSearch® global database.

Apple became stuck with a minuscule, if loyal, share of the PC market, and by the mid-1990s was in very bad financial shape.

When Steve Jobs returned to Apple as CEO in 1997, he axed 70 percent of the development projects, streamlined the firm, and focused on delivering innovative and profitable products (Young and Simon, 2005, p. 262). Most importantly, he orchestrated the introduction in 2001 of the iPod and the iTunes music store that fueled the subsequent surge in CFROI returns and extraordinary gains in shareholder value. Those products represented more than just engineering advancements.

Other firms had tried their hand at bringing digital music players to the marketplace, but were unable to make it an enjoyable experience for customers. To its credit, Apple creatively integrated its hardware, software, and service into a seamless system that delighted customers, and gave Apple the first-mover advantage (favorable CFROI return fade).

It would seem that for Eastman Kodak, IBM, and Apple, missed versus seized opportunities were fundamentally due to ineffective versus effective *ways of thinking*. It appears that culture—unquestioned beliefs as to the right way of doing things that are deeply embedded in an organization's knowledge base—serves a purpose while also creating a problem. One purpose of culture is to facilitate execution of the longstanding business model. The problem is that cultural beliefs can prevent or distort the very feedback that can help craft a much-needed and different business model.

Bethlehem Steel

Over many decades, Bethlehem's management created such an adversarial and poisonous relationship with employees that the end result was an ossified organization whose "DNA" was low productivity and high costs.

Management presided over a bloated bureaucracy that treated itself as royalty. In the late 1950s, seven of the top ten highest-paid executives in the United States worked for Bethlehem. The hugely expensive corporate headquarters building was constructed in the odd shape of a cruciform so that vice presidents could have office windows in two directions—and the list goes on and on (Strohmeyer, 1986).

Foreign companies and U.S. mini-mills developed superior technology at a much faster pace than Bethlehem Steel, and the competitors' employees continuously adopted best practices to improve their productivity. Meanwhile, Bethlehem's unionized workers had negotiated wages that were double those of the average American manufacturing worker. The union contracts also brought incredibly extensive job classifications that were an especially serious drag on productivity.

How did management respond to competitors delivering higher-quality steel at lower prices? A relentless political campaign was waged to "stop illegal steel imports." Keep in mind that companies who buy steel are obviously hurt when their non-U.S. competitors pay a lower global price for steel. In the end, consumers paid higher prices for U.S. products manufactured with steel.

From 1969 to 1992, steel protectionist measures were estimated to have a total cost to consumers in the range of $1,700 to $2,800 (2008 dollars) per American family.[4] This is but one example of the cost of not adhering to free-market principles. As the McKinsey productivity study summarized in Chapter 3 emphasized, consumers benefit from more, not less, competition.

A 2004 article in *Fortune*, "The Sinking of Bethlehem Steel," discussed the union contract changes for six of Bethlehem's plants that were purchased by the International Steel Group after Bethlehem filed for bankruptcy. Job categories were cut from 32 to 5. A machine operator then could replace a light bulb without waiting for an electrician. The *Fortune* reporter asked Jack Welch, widely admired for his skill as the CEO of General Electric, if he could have saved Bethlehem. His reply: "I don't think Christ could have done it" (Loomis, 2004).

The sorry tale of Bethlehem Steel reaffirms the fact that customers, employees, and shareholders have mutual, long-term interests. Political muscle can benefit particular companies or groups of employees for a time, but at a huge, long-term cost to society relative to the presumed benefits. However, this does not address the root cause of economic underperformance. A board staffed by knowledgeable directors with a commitment to represent shareholders could have *forced a fundamental overhaul of business-as-usual practices at Bethlehem at a very early stage.* (See Figure 4.6.)

Nucor

A hallmark of managerial skill is a culture in which employees share in the rewards of productivity and innovation. Employee goals then tend to automatically become aligned with management's productivity goals. In 1962, Ken Iverson became CEO of a failing conglomerate and turned it into Nucor—a uniquely profitable steel company.

Iverson's managerial genius was the implementation of an elegantly simple and effective organizational structure that focused on teamwork, communication, and performance bonuses to achieve extraordinary productivity.

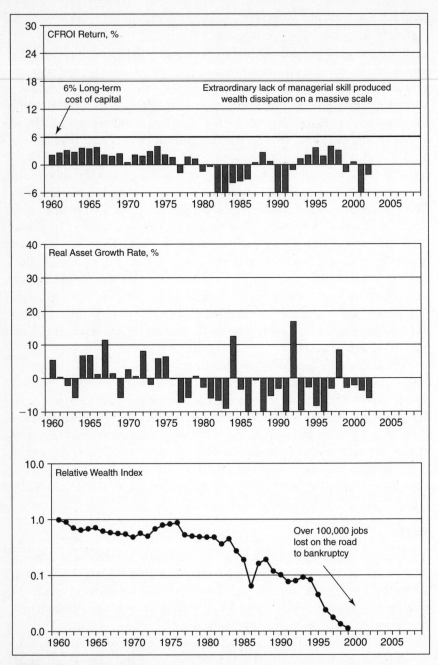

FIGURE 4.6   Bethlehem Steel
Source: Credit Suisse HOLT ValueSearch® global database.

He nurtured the freedom to experiment and learn. Nucor's nonunionized employees have been, by far, the most productive in the steel industry and have consistently earned more than the industry's unionized employees. While the steel industry was undergoing massive layoffs, Nucor never laid off a single employee.

Further, Iverson had decisions about capital equipment purchases made by those in the plants, those responsible for running the equipment. These employees are the ones who continually devise ways to improve efficiency; therefore, they deserve to be rewarded with bonuses for demonstrated productivity improvements. Iverson summarized his approach as follows:

> Concede once and for all that employees, not managers, are the true engines of progress . . . [create] an environment in which employees can stretch for higher and higher levels of performance. . . . Instead of telling people what to do and then hounding them to do it, our managers focus on shaping an environment that frees employees to determine what they can do and should do, to the benefit of themselves and the business.
>
> (Iverson, 1998, p. 98)

How could a small company, such as Nucor in its early years, rapidly gain a significant competitive advantage over its much larger competitors? Clayton Christensen (1997) described how Nucor's development of the mini-mill was a disruptive technology. What mini-mills do is melt scrap steel in electric-arc furnaces, and they thereby avoid the enormous facilities required by integrated mills. Nucor began at the low end of the market, producing the least expensive and lowest-quality steel products (reinforcing bars). Nucor then improved the quality of the steel it produced and moved up-market to steel products with higher-quality requirements. The largest steel companies were already at the high end, focused on customers who used rolled steel that required very high-quality standards (e.g., autos, appliances, and cans).

In 1989, Nucor pioneered yet another major technology—thin-slab casting. Nucor's initial customers did not have the high standards demanded by auto manufacturers and the like. Once again, as with mini-mills, Nucor moved up the learning curve and eventually produced rolled steel to match Big Steel's quality, but at a much lower production cost. Also, the cost of erecting a thin-slab casting plant was a fraction of that for an integrated steel mill. Similar to Bethlehem Steel but in a favorable direction, Nucor demonstrated the fundamental principle that customers, employees, and shareholders have mutual long-term interests. (See Figure 4.7.)

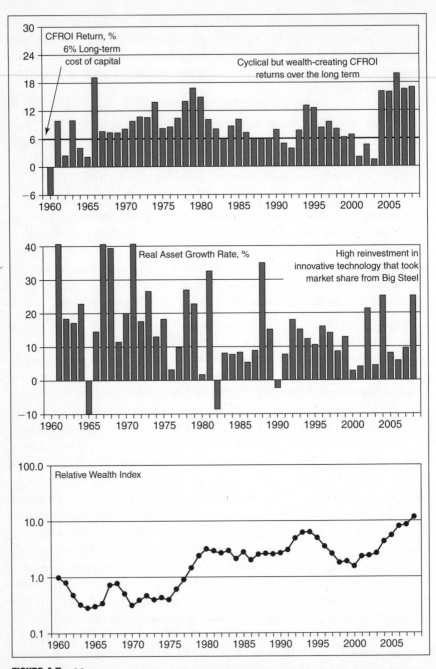

FIGURE 4.7 Nucor
Source: Credit Suisse HOLT ValueSearch® global database.

Kmart

Kmart introduced discount retailing in 1962. This innovation fueled a subsequent surge in CFROI returns (upper panel in Figure 4.8) that resulted in Kmart's stock price outperforming the S&P 500 36-fold from 1960 to 1972 (lower panel). The history of Kmart from 1972 to its bankruptcy in 2002 illustrates a fundamental point: A viable business model must be rooted in a value proposition to customers that is cognizant of *competitive alternatives*.

The Kmart story is encountered repeatedly. It begins with a management that, due to its past success, has gained a command over resources, so it becomes complacent and continues with business as usual. Little attention is given to a radically shifting environment. Often, as with Kmart, management with the board's approval then goes on an acquisition binge to "reposition" their strategy. A smart, effective board (like many private equity boards) would avoid empire building and focus on the core problem. Although rarely done in these situations, one option is to recycle resources to shareholders and shrink the firm—the opposite of an acquisition binge.

While Kmart was being complacent, Sam Walton organized Wal-Mart so as to continually improve upon Kmart's discount retailing concept. During the 1970s and 1980s, the Wal-Mart machine was increasingly outperforming Kmart across the board. Wal-Mart gained distribution efficiency from its store locations; its industry-leading technology revolutionized inventory and supplier processes; and its enthusiastic employees continually worked on all the little details to improve store productivity.

While this was taking place, Kmart greatly expanded its store base with a business-as-usual mindset. Other retail firms, such as Target and Kohl's, developed business models that distinguished their stores from Wal-Mart stores, and thus were able to earn sustained CFROI returns well in excess of the cost of capital. Actually, the Kmart stores were very much like Wal-Mart stores, but in the eyes of customers, not nearly as good. By the beginning of the 1990s, the Wal-Mart machine was at full speed, and Kmart's financial performance was seriously eroded. There was a revolving door of CEOs at Kmart who focused on short-term fixes. Employee morale plummeted.

Kmart's *big-fix* approach was diametrically opposite to that of the steady, relentless, incremental improvements orchestrated at Wal-Mart (Turner, 2003). For example, Kmart belatedly invested huge sums for information technology to catch up to Wal-Mart. Here again, the lack of continuity and effective internal processes hindered Kmart, which had six

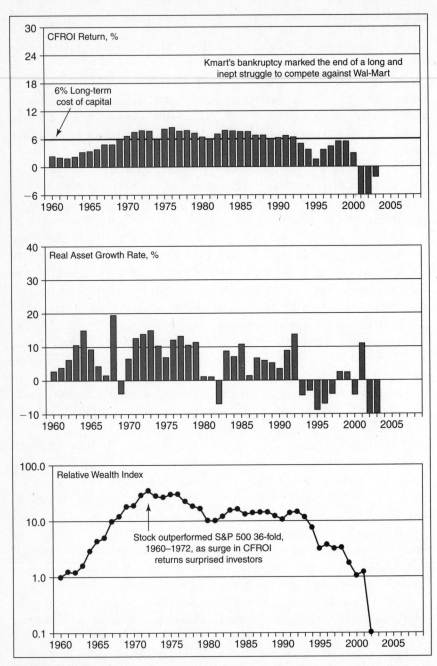

FIGURE 4.8   Kmart
Source: Credit Suisse HOLT ValueSearch® global database.

different CIOs (chief information officers) between 1994 and 2002. Finally, an enormous advantage to Wal-Mart was the exceptional skill and long tenure of its CEO, Sam Walton.

Medtronic

I have a strong hunch that firms that create exceptional shareholder value over longer periods of time, independent of any tailwind from favorable economic shocks, have the benefit of a qualitative factor that is an integral part of managerial skill. That is, these firms are led by CEOs who instill a culture of trust and integrity.

Medtronic, under the leadership of Bill George, is an ideal company to illustrate this point. Bill George was the driving force behind the surge in economic performance and excess shareholder returns (Figure 4.9) during his tenure as CEO from 1991 to 2001. He is widely admired for his leadership skill in general, and in particular, as noted here, for his focus on trust and integrity:

> Under pressure from Wall Street to maximize short-term earnings, boards of directors frequently chose leaders for their charisma instead of their character, their style rather than substance, and their image instead of their integrity. . . . In business, trust is everything, because success depends upon customers' trust in products they buy, employees' trust in their leaders, investors' trust in those who invest for them, and the *public's trust in capitalism.*
>
> (George, 2007, p. xxv, italics added)

Over the years, Medtronic employees were united in a powerful mission to alleviate pain, restore health, and extend life through medical technology. Their first noteworthy innovation was the battery-powered pacemaker in the early 1960s. When Bill George took the helm, his challenge was to instill a performance orientation, that is, to evolve the existing culture into one focused on *efficiently* delivering products to make people's lives better.

Before that, Medtronic's past success had led to complacency, lack of discipline and accountability, conflict avoidance, and rewards for loyalty but not for performance (George, 2003, p. 76). The above-average CFROI returns in the early 1990s would have almost certainly faded downward quickly if a mediocre CEO had been appointed instead of George.

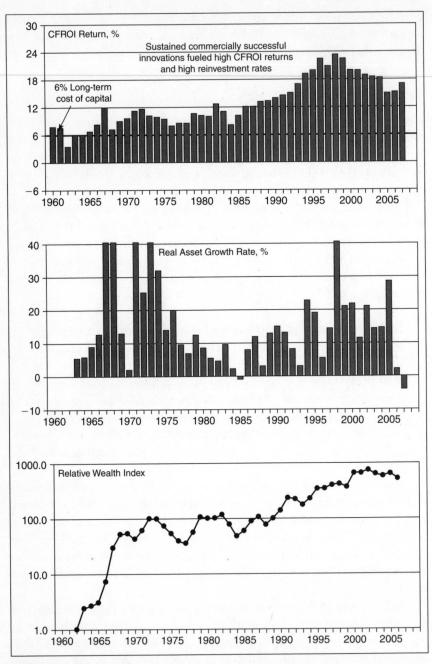

FIGURE 4.9 Medtronic
Source: Credit Suisse HOLT ValueSearch® global database.

In his book, *Authentic Leadership*, George describes how performance must be guided by a fanatical concern for customers who are served in a highly ethical manner:

> One of the greatest challenges of business today is creating a culture that is both values-centered and performance-driven. Many business executives believe they must make trade-offs between the two. I don't buy it. . . . Values begin with telling the truth, internally and externally. Integrity must run deep in the fabric of an organization's culture. It guides the everyday actions of employees and is central to its business conduct. Transparency is an integral part of integrity. The truth, both successes and failures, must be shared openly with the outside world.
>
> (George, 2003, p. 71)

Walgreen Company

In his (2001) mega–best seller, *Good to Great*, Jim Collins describes the superb performance (see Figure 4.10) of Charles R. "Cork" Walgreen III as CEO of Walgreen from 1971 to 1998. I agree with the importance Collins gives to two of Cork Walgreen's accomplishments.

First, he crafted a simple, yet particularly solid, business model that focused Walgreen management on providing exceptional customer convenience through the efficient operation of its drugstores. He purged all non-drugstore operations (Bacon, 2004, pp. 184–186). Clusters of Walgreen drugstores were built in high-traffic areas. Innovations included drive-through pharmacies and a computer system that shared customer pharmacy records with all Walgreen stores.

Second, Cork Walgreen was superb in building and maintaining a highly skilled team of executives to run the firm. That is, he delivered on one of Collins's key criteria for high-performance leadership: "[T]hey *first* got the right people on the bus, the wrong people off the bus, and the right people in the right seats" (Collins, 2001, p. 13).

Cork Walgreen focused on building long-term value, as opposed to Wall Street's concern with quarterly earnings. In the mid-1970s, with inflation skyrocketing, he authorized a switch from FIFO accounting, which was used throughout the industry, to LIFO. This *reduced* accounting earnings, but increased after-tax cash flows (and increased CFROI returns).

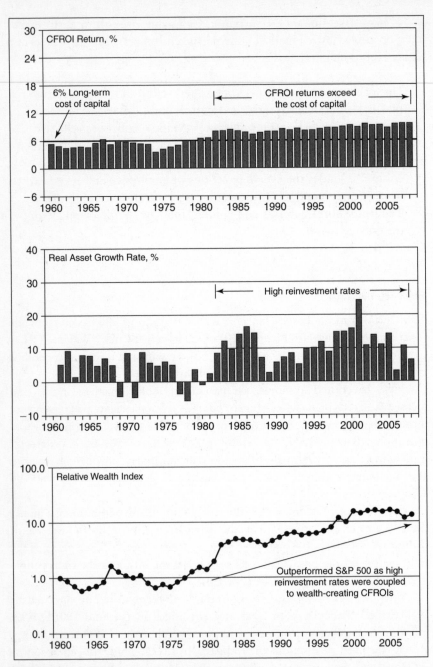

FIGURE 4.10 Walgreen Company
Source: Credit Suisse HOLT ValueSearch® global database.

Walgreen outperformed the S&P 500 10-fold during Cork Walgreen's tenure as CEO. The key was economic performance that exceeded investor expectations. As CFROI returns improved to an above-cost-of-capital level (top panel of Figure 4.10), this achievement was coupled with substantial reinvestment rates (middle panel). The business model scaled. With superb execution, Walgreen dominated Eckerd, its major competitor at that time.

But wealth-creating business models need to adapt to an ever-changing environment: as when different alternatives come on the market for obtaining prescription drugs; as when the competition (CVS Caremark Corp., generic drugs from Wal-Mart) innovates; or when there are diminishing returns, in particular, for new stores. Not only is there a challenge to develop new opportunities, but the degree of difficulty in keeping or gaining competitive advantage usually escalates as a firm grows.

For fiscal 2008, Walgreen had sales of $59 billion and 237,000 employees. A new CEO was hired in 2006, but retired in 2008. During his tenure, substantial acquisitions were made that might offer new growth opportunities (e.g., health clinics). But earnings have trended lower. Management has dramatically lowered its target organic growth rate for new store openings, which seems reasonable. Competition in a free-market economy always poses formidable challenges to firms striving to sustain above-average economic returns and above-average reinvestment rates. And it always benefits consumers.

Donaldson Company

A firm's management must be doing something right in order to survive for almost 100 years as an independent organization and to still be delivering superior economic performance today. Donaldson Company began in 1915 with an air filter product for tractors, and today is a leading worldwide provider of air and liquid filtration systems and replacement parts.

Long-term business success requires skill in providing value to customers and an adaptable business model. As a technology leader in developing filtration products, Donaldson's CFROI returns exceeded the cost of capital from 1963 to 1979, as shown in the top panel of Figure 4.11.

At the beginning of the 1980s, Donaldson's business was heavily tied to heavy-duty diesel engines. Its customers in the agriculture, construction, and heavy truck industries all experienced a severe cyclical downdraft at the same time. As customer demand plummeted, Donaldson's financial performance got hammered.

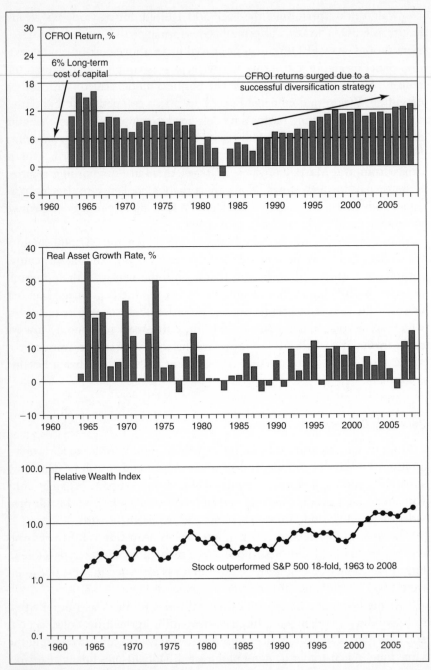

FIGURE 4.11 Donaldson Company
Source: Credit Suisse HOLT ValueSearch® global database.

Importantly, Donaldson's management reorganized the firm and developed a strategy of "focused diversification." Donaldson had in place a compelling value proposition in that it had an R&D track record of producing innovative filters that solved critical customer needs and thereby justified their premium prices and above-average profitability. The new strategy was to expand this value proposition to a much wider customer base by leveraging its technology, customer relationships, and global presence.

As the new strategy was implemented, including acquisitions of smaller firms that fit the new strategic direction, CFROI returns steadily improved. The firm continued to develop innovative customer solutions typically by delivering smaller filters with far greater performance. Customer applications became increasingly diverse, ranging from filter applications for huge gas turbines to hard disk drives.

Since the decade of the 1980s, the steadiness of Donaldson's CFROI returns through subsequent downturns in the economy attests to management's diversification success. Donaldson outperformed the S&P 500 handily from 1990 to 2008 as it transformed itself from a cyclical U.S.-based company into a highly diversified global company.

Donaldson is a well-managed, midsized company ($2.2 billion in sales in 2008) whose CEOs have long tenure and build value for shareholders by providing value to customers. This type of management culture is diametrically opposed to the mindset of CEOs who build empires through mega-sized acquisitions that are not grounded in value to the customer.

LIFE-CYCLE OBSERVATIONS

Boards of directors, managements, and the general investing public develop rules of thumb for what they think drives stock prices. Firms' stock prices that deliver big gains over a number of years typically correlate with high growth rates in sales and earnings. Given this, the usual management strategy to "grow the business" is viewed by many as beneficial to shareholders. Similarly, short-term moves in stock prices are highly correlated with announcements of quarterly earnings that are above or below Wall Street's expectations. Hence, many assume that management's goal should be to meet, or preferably exceed, quarterly earnings expectations.

However, these rules of thumb make for a faulty valuation model. For example, the previously illustrated Bethlehem Steel track record is a prime example of how wealth can be dissipated by reinvestment ("growth") in a below-cost-of-capital business. The key issue is actually competitive fade. Managements need to develop strategies that can *sustain* favorable economic returns, even if this entails a reinvestment rate that appears to be overly conservative and keeps the firm from being classified as a "growth stock." *Growth stock* is a vague term that leads to unclear thinking and should be purged from one's investment vocabulary.

To study life-cycle charts is to study how wealth is created or destroyed over the long term. One develops a deep appreciation of how difficult it is for a firm to sustain superior economic performance in the face of relentless competition and a continually changing business environment. To excel and achieve a favorable competitive fade, all of the firm's employees, including upper levels of management, need to learn quickly and use that knowledge to improve the firm's core processes relentlessly. The problem with top management having an extreme focus on quarterly earnings is that this can easily result in a lack of attention to improving those critical processes that in fact drive the firm's long-term financial performance.

Moreover, a firm's current culture has coalesced around its "ways of doing things" that generated success in the past. But if these old, ingrained processes are not tightly linked to providing value to the customer and not adaptable to changes in the environment, then at some point competitors will offer a better value to customers. IBM and Digital Equipment got into this bind.

Life-cycle track records are the right scorecard to link management decisions to long-term wealth creation or dissipation. Such track records offer a viable alternative to misguided rules of thumb that can too easily encourage bad management and investment decisions.

To sum up, boards, CEOs, and investors often talk about long-term wealth creation, but actually look at the world through a short-term accounting lens. Life-cycle track records are a far more useful lens.

Summary of Key Ideas

- Applied to the long-term histories of companies, the competitive life-cycle framework provides an economic basis for understanding levels and changes in stock prices over time. Managerial skill and competition are the primary determinants of firms' long-term performance.

- The market value of a firm's equity and debt represents the present value of an anticipated long-term, net cash receipt stream that is generated by the firm's anticipated life-cycle performance. That life-cycle performance is the product of four variables: economic returns, costs of capital, reinvestment rates, and fade rates.

■ It is helpful to view the setting of market prices as a process of investors assessing firms' past life-cycle track records and forecasting likely future life-cycle performance. Experience with life-cycle track records not only provides investment insights grounded in sound economics but also encourages users to abandon the use of vague and misleading terms such as *growth stock* and *value stock*.

■ Many institutional money management organizations have benefited from implementation of the life-cycle framework. Benefits include the ability to quickly analyze a company's history, to pinpoint key valuation issues, and to make improved judgments of likely future corporate performance. Short-term information, such as quarterly reports, is analyzed within a long-term perspective.

■ Many investors and business managers who have not worked with life-cycle track records employ a rule-of-thumb theory of stock prices drawn from their experiences. Consequently, earnings-per-share growth rates and quarterly earnings surprises play a dominant role in their valuation models. Such models are poor guides for either insightful investment research or sound management decision making.

CHAPTER 5

The Life-Cycle Valuation Model as a Total System

Finance scholars have long embraced the notion that we advance faster and better by first *creating theories that make predictions about the way the world works.* Next *we turn to the data to see if the numbers conform to the predictions. If we find that they do not, we either (a) "refine" the theories, by altering the assumptions upon which they are based, or (b) "refine" the empirical tests until the data speaks in a voice we can* appreciate and understand. . . . *But most of the major advances in the frontier of human knowledge did not follow an arrow running through the theories into the empirical tests.* Rather, *most of* our greatest triumphs proceeded in the opposite direction from data to theory. *The arrow goes from straightforward empirical observation to the development of theories which give us the insights to understand* what we have seen.

—Robert Haugen, *The New Finance: The Case Against Efficient Markets (emphasis in original)*

This chapter deals with important technical issues concerning the development and application of the life-cycle valuation model. This material is not critical to understanding the ideas covered in the other chapters in this book. Yet readers not especially interested in technical details might find it interesting to learn about the evolution of a unique commercial research program that produced a valuation model, global database, and life-cycle way of thinking that is widely used by institutional money managers.[1] Of particular interest is that this research yielded highly advanced procedures to measure investor expectations, which are critical to any common stock investment decision and even to one's investment philosophy.

EFFICIENT MARKETS VERSUS BEHAVIORAL FINANCE

It is not uncommon for an investor to hear the question: Do you believe in some form of efficient markets in which most, if not all, relevant information about a firm's future is embedded in its current stock price, or do you subscribe to behavioral finance, which stresses emotional biases and less-than-rational pricing of stocks? Presented as mutually exclusive options, the question is flawed. The life-cycle valuation model enables investors to appreciate the arguments for both efficient markets and behavioral finance.

On one hand, experience working with company life-cycle track records and investor expectations leads to a recognition that, on average over long time periods, it is exceedingly difficult to "outforecast" the market and consistently earn investor returns, adjusted for risk, that substantially exceed the market return. On the other hand, the ability to fine tune investor expectations of firms' future life cycles shows that extreme pessimism and optimism are frequently encountered. At such times in particular, one may have genuine insights about firms' long-term prospects that are not accurately reflected in current stock prices, and that can be used to make rewarding buy and sell decisions.

One constant is that the investors' task is always difficult since a firm's future can involve a wide distribution of possible outcomes. Individual firms can exceed even very optimistic expectations and disappoint even exceptionally dire expectations. Experienced investors know this all too well.

By way of background, the late Chuck Callard and I started Callard, Madden & Associates (CMA) in 1969 as a research firm focused on the needs of institutional money managers. Shortly thereafter, I began to work full time on a "model corporation" project to develop an improved DCF (discounted cash flow) valuation model. That work also produced the CFROI metric for estimating a firm's economic returns. This early research used the life-cycle framework reviewed in Chapter 4 and eventually became known as the *CFROI valuation model*.

Meanwhile, Chuck did a great deal of analysis of macroeconomic time series related to stock market trends. His research on the intertwined effects of inflation and personal tax rates for capital gains and dividends on the equity investors' demanded return (cost of equity capital) was never published as a journal article, but was far ahead of mainstream finance in this area.

This commercial research program was expanded and carried forward by HOLT Value Associates, which was formed by four of my ex-CMA partners. My 1999 book, *CFROI Valuation: A Total System Approach to Valuing the Firm*, laid out the technical details of the model as it was constructed at that time. HOLT was acquired by Credit Suisse in 2002.

For decades, the CFROI valuation model has benefited from an intense feedback loop between HOLT's research staff and its worldwide institutional money manager clients who have a vested interest in improving the accuracy of the valuation model and the company track record displays for a database that currently contains approximately 20,000 companies in over 60 countries. One way to summarize this research effort is in terms of key questions asked and corresponding answers that build on one another in a logical sequence.

The remainder of this chapter is organized according to the key questions listed here and answers that often differ in important ways from mainstream finance.

- What are the fundamental principles used to construct the valuation model?
- What are the units of measurement for the model components?
- How is the investor's discount rate, or the firm's cost of capital, estimated?
- What is the process for improving the model itself and the inputs used by it?
- How are investor expectations used in making buy, hold, and sell decisions?
- What are the implications of the life-cycle way of thinking for critical conceptual accounting issues?

VALUATION MODEL PRINCIPLES

All conceptually sound DCF valuation models apply a discount rate to a forecasted stream of cash receipts. The life-cycle model values the total firm—that is, both the equity and debt capital owners. Their receipts are labeled *net cash receipts (NCRs)*—cash inflows less cash outflows over time for needed reinvestment in the business.

Much of the academic work on valuation is focused on mathematical ways to articulate a forecast of cash receipts, with a notable disregard for how one develops insights and ways of assessing the plausibility of forecasts from analysis of historical data. The early thinking at CMA gave utmost importance to using historical data to better understand the past in order to make better forecasts of the future.

Consider a firm's track record, as illustrated in Chapter 4, as representing a company's up-to-date history. A forecast of a company's long-term, future life cycle is an intuitive way to generate a future NCR stream—that is, NCRs implied by the forecast economic returns and reinvestment rates applied to today's asset base. Figure 5.1 packages this process in terms of a warranted value that is calculated as the present value warranted by a particular forecast of a firm's future life cycle and by the assigned discount rate. Although not necessary for the discussion in this chapter, a more detailed version of Figure 5.1 would specify NCRs from existing assets and, separately, NCRs from future investments.

As a total system, all the variables in Figure 5.1 are interrelated. How one specifies operating assets influences the calculations for economic returns and reinvestment rates. Consequently, the observed historical fade rates for economic returns and asset growth rates (proxy for reinvestment rates) also depend on the specification of operating assets. For example, the life-cycle

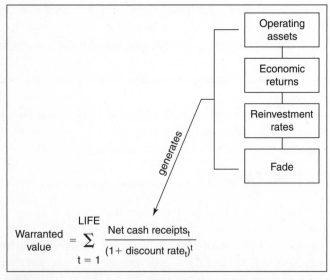

FIGURE 5.1 Life-Cycle Valuation Model

track record for a typical pharmaceutical company is significantly different if R&D expenditures are, or are not, capitalized and included in operating assets. Also true, but less obvious, is that the assignment of a company-specific discount rate should be logically consistent with the NCR forecasting procedures used.

Figure 5.1 shows economic returns as one component of the process that generates NCRs. It is a gross understatement to say that economic returns are important to valuation. A fundamental wealth-creation principle is that investments that yield economic returns above (below) the investors' discount rate, or cost of capital, create (destroy) wealth.

Let's define more carefully what we mean by an economic return. Consider a project with cash outflows followed by after-tax cash inflows, inclusive of recovery of the value of nondepreciating assets at the end of the project's life. The achieved internal rate of return for this project is its economic return. If the outflows and inflows have not been adjusted for changes in the purchasing power of the monetary unit, it is a nominal economic return. If all outflows and inflows are expressed in monetary units of the same purchasing power (e.g., dollars of purchasing power of a specified year), it is a real economic return.

Note that a nominal return of 8 percent with 0 percent inflation provides a real 8 percent return, whereas the same nominal return of 8 percent coupled to 8 percent inflation provides a 0 percent real return. This is quite significant. With an 8 percent real return, wealth doubles in nine years compared to no change for a 0 percent real return.

It is reasonable to expect that equity investors set stock prices with expectations of achieving a specified *real* return after anticipated payments for any personal taxes on dividends and capital gains (Madden, 1999, pp. 86–87; Sialm, 2006). With this line of reasoning, when investors experience an increase in their real tax burden, they should demand a higher cost of capital from corporations (stock prices drop) as compensation in order to maintain their real, net-of-personal-tax return goal.

Real economic returns for projects were at the heart of my model corporation work at CMA. Input to the model included period-by-period economic returns for specific projects and reinvestment rates. Output included balance sheets and income statements. The model corporation software was written to represent the firm as a portfolio of projects. Those projects had specified characteristics: economic life for depreciable assets, proportion of nondepreciating assets released at the end of the project, plus a real economic return that determined period-by-period, after-tax cash inflows. New investment in the form of capital expenditures and additional net working capital in each period represented the start of a new project to replace a project completed in that period. The amounts for new investment conformed to the specified real, reinvestment rate, which also involved targeted proportions for debt in the capital structure and dividend payouts from earnings.

This view of the firm as a portfolio of ongoing projects is depicted in Figure 5.2. A project consisted of an initial investment outlay (down arrow) followed by cash inflows (up arrows) over the life of the project, including a final release of any nondepreciating assets. The income statement at a point in time, such as 2008, represented cash inflows from prior projects that were still productive in 2008. The 2008 gross plant account consisted of past capital expenditures for not-yet-completed projects. Also on the balance sheet were nondepreciating assets, such as net working capital and land, from past projects.

The above perspective illustrates the commonsense intuition that the value of existing assets, at year-end 2008, depends on the wind-down pattern of anticipated cash inflows in years 2009 to 2011 (right-hand side of Figure 5.2). This figure also provides an intuition about the origin of the CFROI metric. *The CFROI is calculated as a project ROI using aggregate data from the financial statements.* The initial down arrow is gross plant plus nondepreciating assets, followed by equal cash inflows, or up arrows, over the average economic life of the assets, and a final up arrow for release of nondepreciating

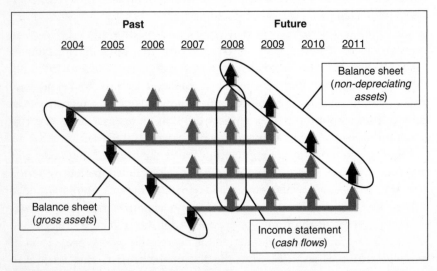

FIGURE 5.2 The Firm as a Portfolio of Projects

assets. It made sense to keep these variables in plain sight because of the multitude of accounting issues that can give a significantly distorted picture of economic reality (e.g., accelerated depreciation). For an updated technical discussion of CFROI returns, see Larsen and Holland (2008).[2]

The CFROI framework has proven very useful for identifying and solving issues in which accounting treatments differed from business economics (i.e., economic reality). A small sample of such issues include: capitalization of R&D expenses, operating lease capitalization, acquisition intangibles, financial subsidiaries, off-balance-sheet liabilities, special items, stock option expenses, franchise rights, asset impairments, and the list goes on.

Consider an economic perspective for the straight-line accounting treatment for depreciation charges. The productive capacity of plant and equipment does not decline nearly as rapidly as implied by straight-line depreciation (Thomas and Atra, 2009). This depreciation assumption operates behind the scenes in the calculation of a conventional *RONA (return on net assets)*. Plant and equipment that is substantially depreciated yet fully operational is carried at full historical cost in the gross plant account but has a minuscule value in the net plant account. Based on gross plant value, the CFROI return is not distorted in such situations, whereas a conventional RONA is too high. Those who prefer the use of a RONA metric should calculate depreciation charges in a manner that overcomes the inadequacy of straight-line depreciation.

Much care is needed in analyzing how a firm's business economics translate to the mathematics of a model's present value calculations. Consider the handling of a firm's existing assets. Recall that the warranted value of a firm is the present value of NCRs from both existing assets and future investments.

Quantifying the value of future investments implied in current stock prices is important and is calculated as the total market value of debt and equity less the estimated present value of existing assets. The proportion of a firm's total market value due to future investments can be interpreted as an indicator of competitive advantage. The closer the estimated value of existing assets is to economic reality, the more accurate will be the implied value of future investments.

A relevant example would be the analysis of a potential acquisition of an oil and gas exploration company. Would it not make sense to first estimate the present value of the wind-down of NCRs from existing (proven) reserves? Next, separately assess the value of future investments from drilling new wells on owned or leased properties with more uncertain prospects and from new discoveries due to the exploration skill of the firm.

Mainstream finance has popularized two ways to treat existing assets that ignore the cash flow wind-down approach, yet are mathematically correct within the context of a particular valuation model. One approach is to estimate a normalized level of earnings and treat it as a perpetual annuity. This necessitates the assumption that depreciation charges are automatically reinvested every year in the future regardless of the level of economic return achieved. This also puts a considerable amount of future investments into the present value calculation of today's existing assets. The other approach is to use a book value for today's assets regardless of the level of economic return being achieved on those assets.

We should not lose sight of the role of a valuation model as a thinking template for strategic options. A focus on explicit cash flows from existing assets raises the relevant question as to whether certain assets might have a higher value to a different owner better able to generate higher cash flows from these assets in the future. For management in particular, the present value computations for existing assets should focus on the wind-down pattern of cash flows.[3] The annuity approach and book value approach simplify the mathematics of a valuation model at the cost of obscuring economic reality for those who let their thinking follow the logic of their valuation model.

MEASUREMENT UNITS

Of the myriad issues concerning accounting treatments that induce measurement problems for estimating economic returns, let's focus on one rather important variable—changes in the purchasing power of the monetary unit over time, which is generally labeled either *inflation or deflation*. To address this issue, the model corporation was set up to utilize an input time series of inflation/deflation in addition to the input life-cycle variables of *real* economic returns and *real* reinvestment rates.

Mainstream finance research on valuation tends to ignore this issue under the assumption that it makes no difference whether one uses nominal or real numbers, as long as one is consistent in the application. In other words, it's no big deal.

Well, it is a big deal, if, for example, one is concerned with accuracy in observing firms' track records. *The mistake is to assume that accounting-derived measures of profitability are simple nominal numbers.* Put differently, would an engineer divide 12 inches by 3 feet and say the answer is 4? In a similar vein, the plant account for an industrial firm has vintages of prior additions expressed in purchasing power units for the year in which the capital expenditures were made. The balance sheet figure for the plant account therefore is not in current dollars for the year represented by the balance sheet. Such an asset figure cannot meaningfully be compared to cash flows in current dollars when the past environment has significant changes in the purchasing power of the monetary unit. This becomes a very big deal when one draws inferences from observed patterns of accounting-derived ROIs or discount rates over long time periods or across countries.

The CFROI metric incorporates adjustments so that it is a *real* measure that approximates the average *real* economic returns being achieved from a firm's portfolio of ongoing projects. The key adjustment is a markup of assets to current dollar amounts to match cash flows expressed in current dollars.

As a practical matter, is it worth the effort to strive for consistency in measurement units? An application of the model corporation addressed this question by inputting a time series of repetitive 6 percent real project ROIs and 2 percent real reinvestment rates, project characteristics similar to the average S&P 500 industrial firm, and similar financial leverage. One example illustrated in Figure 5.3 used data from 1875 to 1995 for nominal interest rates and for the GDP Deflator series to reflect levels of inflation/deflation.[4]

Figure 5.3 plots the calculated CFROI returns from modeled annual financial statements, and these CFROI returns match the repetitive 6 percent real economic returns being achieved on all projects. For comparison purposes, the popular Earnings/Common Equity was calculated. As a levered ROI metric, one would expect its values to be a bit higher than the 6 percent real project ROIs. But the actual plot of the simulated Earnings/Common Equity is a wildly gyrating line going from a low of 3 percent to a high of 20 percent, essentially due to the variation in a single variable—the purchasing power of the dollar. Lessons learned from studies of long-term competitive fade, covering the time period of Figure 5.3, would be a bit misleading, to say the least, using a rubber ruler of Earnings/Common Equity as a measuring stick.

A few more points about this model corporation work relevant for security analysis in general and, in particular, for how finance students learn about valuation deserve attention. Those involved with discounted cash flow valuation models should gain absolute clarity on the calculation of net cash receipts (Madden, 1999, p. 68). NCRs can be calculated from the firm's perspective (cash flows from operations less reinvestment). The

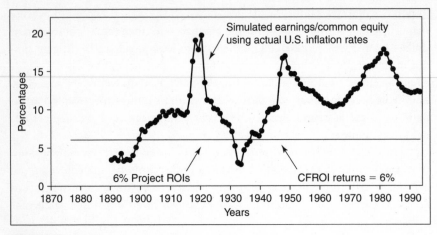

FIGURE 5.3 CFROI versus Earnings/Common Equity
Source: Madden (1996), exhibit 4.

identical NCRs can be calculated from the perspective of the capital owners (dividends, share repurchases, interest payments, and debt repayments less stock sales and new debt issuance). The above is important because "free cash flows" are often used as a substitute for NCRs and there are numerous definitions in use for *free cash flow*.

When the model corporation software is properly programmed, an accurate warranted value is calculated each period based on future NCRs. This can be verified in that the achieved equity investor return (dividends plus capital gains), year-by-year, equals the equity cost of capital. This is a useful exercise, for finance students especially, to see how the entire process checks out: forecasting life-cycle variables, generating NCRs, calculating warranted values, and proving that the present value computations are accurate. A particularly revealing model corporation exercise for students would be to calculate a CFROI return or adjusted RONA from as-reported financial statements that mirrors the repetitive real project ROIs. This requires one to understand how to make adjustments for inflation and deflation.

Simulation, along the lines of the model corporation work, deserves more academic attention in order to address the most difficult and important measurement challenges (e.g., intangibles) in connecting business economics to accounting data, and then to valuation. A good example is the simulation work of Healy, Myers, and Howe (2002) that addressed the complex issues of R&D capitalization.

FORWARD-LOOKING, MARKET-DERIVED DISCOUNT RATES

With a total system perspective for Figure 5.1, it is apparent that *risk* could be handled in the numerator (as adjustments to NCRs) or the denominator (adjustment to the discount rate). That is, a higher risk penalty could be assessed with a harsher fade for economic returns and reinvestment rates. Or, the risk could be put into a higher discount rate alone.

This systems mindset leads one to the conclusion that the assignment of a discount rate is dependent on the procedures used to forecast NCRs. This is particularly relevant to models incorporating standard ways of forecasting future fade rates based on company characteristics.[5] In contrast, mainstream finance relies on either a capital asset pricing model (CAPM)–*based calculation for the discount rate or some other twist to the CAPM theory. These discount rates are then parachuted into valuation models without regard to how users make NCR forecasts.*

A helpful approach to the topic of forward-looking discount rates is to observe how discount rates are handled in the bond market. For bonds, the anticipated NCR streams are composed of interest and principal payments. Knowing today's price for a bond enables one to calculate a *yield-to-maturity (YTM)*—that is, the implied discount rate.

Consider a group of bonds with known credit quality ratings that are about to be sold to investors. Our objective is to estimate the discount rates that will be assigned by investors as implied in the soon-to-be-traded market prices for these bonds. These estimates could be obtained from a regression equation developed from a large universe of publicly traded bonds. For this universe of bonds, we would record YTM observations as the dependent variable and credit quality ratings as the independent variable.

For the group of soon-to-be-traded bonds, we could then use this regression equation to estimate forward-looking, market-derived discount rates. We can apply the exact same methodology to stocks, even though future NCRs are substantially more difficult to forecast for stocks than for bonds. Similar to credit quality ratings being the dominant variable determining demanded discount rates in the bond market, there are two variables for stocks that are logical choices and have proven to consistently have a dominant influence on the investors' discount rates (Madden, 1998), which are weighted averages of firms' equity and debt discount rates.

The first variable is financial leverage. Note that CFROI returns are calculated using after-tax cash flows, which reflect the tax-deductible benefit of interest payments. But there is an offset to this benefit. As financial leverage increases, equity investors should require a higher return to compensate for a higher risk of financial difficulties. It is clear that high leverage played a significant role in crushing the common stock values of numerous firms during the 2008–2009 housing and credit crisis.

The second variable is company size, based on the plausible assumption that investors demand a higher return from smaller, less liquid companies' stocks. This is due to both higher transactions costs in buying and selling positions in smaller companies and elevated business risk that cannot be diversified away.

A recent experience with Taiwanese companies serves as an excellent example of the benefit of a systems mindset for market-derived, forward-looking discount rates. In a systems approach, learning is a function of identifying problems and developing solutions by paying attention to interactions among variables. Along these lines, a (2006) Credit Suisse HOLT report, authored by Ng, Jhaveri, and Graziano, described a major improvement for Taiwanese companies.

Let's begin with problem recognition. The aggregate market-derived discount rate for Taiwanese companies seemed implausibly high. Also, Taiwanese companies with low financial leverage had *higher* discount rates than the high-leverage companies—a result that did not make economic sense.

The root cause of these problems was identified as excessively high CFROI returns for the many companies that generously dispensed shares for employee stock bonuses. From the shareholders' perspective, this outlay was clearly an economic expense, although it was ignored in computing accounting net income.[6] This artificially boosted market-derived discount rates.

Figure 5.1 is helpful in understanding this point. Substitute a firm's known market value for the warranted value. The market value can be matched by either one of the following:

- Discounting higher NCRs (boosted by ignoring employee stock bonuses) at a higher rate
- Discounting lower NCRs (this is more accurate) at a lower rate

The solution was to incorporate an appropriate charge for employee stock bonuses. This lowered cash flow used in calculating CFROI returns. With the new, lower CFROI returns (better reflecting business economics), calculated market-derived discount rates declined. Interestingly, technology companies were the biggest users of employee stock bonuses and these companies also tend to have low financial leverage. Thus, the CFROI fix also resolved the problem of a too-high discount rate for low-leverage companies. Finally, there was an across-the-board improvement in the tracking of warranted values with actual stock prices for all Taiwanese companies.

PROBLEMS WITH CAPM COST OF CAPITAL

With its elegant mathematics grounded in the neoclassical economic principles of *equilibrium, rationality*, and *efficient markets*, the CAPM has extraordinarily deep roots in mainstream finance. In general, finance textbooks (Brealey, Myers, and Allen, 2006 is an example) explain portfolio construction in terms of investors striving to achieve higher expected returns for a given level of risk. The CAPM is an integral part of this explanation and has become a foundation for thinking about stock prices.

The CAPM was brought into discounted cash flow valuation of individual firms as the basis for estimating a firm's equity cost of capital. According to the CAPM, a firm's equity discount rate equals the risk-free rate plus the product of a stock's *Beta* (i.e., volatility) multiplied by the risk premium of the overall equity market (i.e., expected excess return of the equity market over the risk-free rate). This is the standard method for estimating a firm's equity cost of capital taught to finance students.

One objection to market-derived discount rates replacing CAPM rates is the necessity of maintaining a monitored database, similar to the database maintained by Credit Suisse HOLT. Fair enough; but increased valuation accuracy through more appropriate company-specific discount rates can generate big rewards.

The other major objection is that the market-derived discount rate methodology described in this chapter can produce "illogical" discount rates. For example, consider a technology company and a food company that have approximately the same financial leverage and the same liquidity (company size). The regression procedure used in the life-cycle model for estimating company-specific discount rates would give the same discount rate to both companies. Yet, as critics point out, everyone "knows" that food companies have a lower cost of capital than technology companies because food companies have more stable and predictable cash flows and lower Betas than technology companies.

The accusation of illogic reveals an inability to think outside the CAPM framework. The life-cycle valuation model's standard fade forecast for a typical technology company is much less favorable compared to that of a typical food company. A technology company with above-cost-of-capital, but highly variable, economic returns and/or high reinvestment rates would be assigned a faster downward fade compared to a food company, which typically has more stable economic returns and slower reinvestment rates.[7] The life-cycle approach handles the "risk" difference in the numerator.

To sum up, there are three reasons for preferring some form of a market-derived discount rate instead of a CAPM/Beta discount rate. First, to repeat, a discount rate that is estimated consistent with the procedures for forecasting NCRs should be preferred over a CAPM/Beta discount rate that is essentially parachuted into any and all valuation models.

Second, a *forward-looking* discount rate should be preferred over a discount rate, such as CAPM/Beta, that is based on historical data and incapable of adjusting for near-term changes in the environment (inflation expectations, new tax legislation, etc.).

Third, application of the CAPM equation requires two inputs that are notoriously difficult to judge—Beta and the equity market risk premium over the risk-free rate. These are applied as forward-looking variables but they are necessarily estimated from historical data.

Depending on the past time periods selected, a stock's Beta could easily range from say 1.2 to 1.5 and the market premium could easily range from say 4 to 7 percent. Users of CAPM have little to guide them in the selection of these two critical inputs. Combining a risk-free rate of 3 percent with a Beta of 1.2 and a 4 percent market premium yields a 7.8 percent equity cost of capital. In contrast, substitution of a Beta of 1.5 and a market premium of 7 percent yields a 13.5 percent equity cost of capital.

The valuation impact of using a 7.8 or 13.5 percent equity cost of capital is enormous. A similar big impact on an economic value added, or EVA® (trademark of Stern Stewart & Co.), calculation occurs when the equity cost of capital is estimated with the CAPM equation or alternative procedures, such as arbitrage pricing theory or the Fama-French three-factor model that is increasingly being used by quantitative portfolio managers (Fabozzi, Focardi, and Jones, 2008). In practice, market-derived discount rates for sample of companies have a much smaller range than CAPM/Beta discount rates.

IMPROVING THE VALUATION PROCESS

Mainstream finance has not embraced a market-derived discount rate approach due, in part, to the difficulty in calculating investor expectations for firms' future NCRs. In contrast, from the early CMA work to today's Credit Suisse HOLT global research program, a broad database of monitored forecast NCRs has been maintained and continually improved. The improvements are principally accounting adjustments for more accurate CFROI returns and improved forecasts of long-term fade rates.

This process of improvement is a good example of the PAK Loop in operation. Critical to effective cycles of perceiving, acting, and knowing is the use of long-term charts that plot annual, warranted equity values alongside firms' actual stock prices over time. These warranted value charts plus the valuation model (Figure 5.1) and the life-cycle track records (Chapter 4) are the basic tools for researching the causes of levels and changes in stock prices over time.

These three tools are used in an unending cycle of problem identification and resolution. Typically, a potential problem is observed as a systematic under- or over-tracking of warranted versus actual stock prices for a firm. The source of the problem is tracked down using the valuation components of Figure 5.1. For example, a firm's per-share warranted equity values might be substantially below its actual stock price, year after year. Perhaps the accounting life (calculated as gross plant divided by depreciation charges) used as a proxy for economic life is clearly too short because of accelerated depreciation charges. Using a longer life that more closely fits economic reality would increase the value of existing assets. And it also would increase CFROI returns and lead to a higher value for future investments. This fix would move warranted values closer to actual stock prices.

Confidence in implementing a fix increases when there is a compelling economic reason for adjusting the accounting data. Also, confidence increases when other firms with the same issue show substantial tracking improvement after the fix is applied to their data.

The calculation, at a point in time, of a warranted value requires a company-specific discount rate and a long-term NCR forecast. The assignment of a discount rate has already been discussed. As to the NCR forecast, the more critical issue is the long-term fade pattern of CFROI returns. Think of a five-year window of future CFROI returns where the +1-year CFROI return is tied to security analysts' EPS forecasts and the +5-year CFROI return is

calculated from an assigned fade rate according to observed company characteristics. After the fifth year, CFROI returns are forecasted to regress toward
the long-term cost of capital level.[8]

Life-cycle empirical research (Madden, 1996) on company characteristics and fade rates was based on the underlying assumptions about the
interplay between managerial skill and competition described in Chapter 4.[9]
Here are some highlights of observed patterns and reasons based on life-
cycle interpretations.

The higher the CFROI level, the faster will be the fade. This is due to
competitors seeking to obtain a share of this wealth-creation opportunity.
High CFROI returns coupled with high reinvestment rates lead to fast fade
rates because (1) big reinvestment rates signal a big product market opportunity, which is especially attractive to competitors, and (2) the degree of
difficulty in managing a business that is experiencing rapid growth necessarily increases. All else equal, above-average CFROI return firms with low
year-to-year variability in their CFROI returns fade more slowly. This makes
sense since the more controlled the firm's operations, the more likely that
higher managerial skill is involved. Finally, firms with above-average CFROI
returns tend to fade down, those with average (cost of capital) CFROI returns
tend to stick at that level, and below-average CFROI firms tend to fade up
due to pressure on management to improve, shrink the business, or both.

Over many years of research and feedback from knowledgeable users,
the procedures for forecasting NCRs have improved, leading to closer tracking of warranted versus actual stock prices. This process produces NCR
forecasts that, on average, more and more closely mirror investor expectations. Consequently, as the universe of companies expands and contains
better proxies for investor NCR expectations, the market-derived discount
rates also become more accurate.

Keep in mind that these discount rates are attuned to the fade forecasting procedures used—a total system approach. Users of the valuation model
are familiar with the standard fade forecasts based on company characteristics. When making their own judgments about a company's future performance, they pay particular attention to the standard fade forecast versus
the fade forecast implied in today's stock price as a gauge of the market's
current degree of pessimism or optimism.

The learning tasks described above are rooted in fast and effective cycles
through the PAK Loop. As described in the opening chapter, these cycles do
not have a "start point." One's knowledge base affects how the world is
perceived and what constitutes a problem that interferes with achieving a

purpose or an anomaly showing a deficiency in an existing assumption or theory. Dealing with problems and testing hypotheses provides critical feedback that in turn affects one's knowledge base. This loop perspective avoids having to prefer an inductive or deductive methodology since both are at work in cycles through the PAK Loop.

In sharp contrast to the above, Robert Haugen's quote at the beginning of this chapter accurately portrays mainstream finance's reverence for elegant theory that sets the direction for subsequent empirical work. For example, many mainstream finance researchers rely heavily on top-down (deductive) theory such as market efficiency and the CAPM. In the past, the strong pull of this dominant view impeded experimentation with variables that might jeopardize the market efficiency and the CAPM constructs. Note how long it took for behavioral finance articles to be published in top-tier journals.

Modern finance researchers by and large have used the CAPM to guide much of their work. An elegant explanation of a mathematically logical relationship between expected returns on stocks and risk, the CAPM provides a blueprint, given its assumptions, for investors to optimize their portfolios to the highest expected return for a given level of risk. Notwithstanding the CAPM's poor empirical record of predictability (Fama and French, 2004) and its challengeable assumptions, it continues to exert a strong hold on mainstream finance.[10]

Increasingly, behavioral finance researchers have presented serious challenges to the premises and empirical underpinnings of mainstream finance theory (Thaler, 2005). But proponents of the status quo seem little concerned about dealing with the weaknesses of their theory. Rather, they take the offensive, asking, Where is the better theory? Believing none has been offered as yet, the core body of knowledge presented in finance textbooks and taught to finance students has not been significantly changed. Thus the dominant theory remains intact.

Early on, the accepted goal of the life-cycle research program became to better understand *levels* and *changes* in company stock prices on a global basis so portfolio managers could make better investment decisions. In contrast, mainstream finance was focused on a logically consistent equilibrium model that related risk to expected return—and the CAPM became the answer. It was not designed to explain the level of firms' market prices, but rather to explain the *change* in prices that drive investor returns.

Strong beliefs in market efficiency and the CAPM were never a part of the life-cycle work. Nevertheless, those involved with the research gained a great appreciation for the market's ability to see through complex accounting issues and, most of the time, to astutely anticipate firms' future profitability. An integral part of the life-cycle research was a knowledge-building process focused on anomalies. The research was designed to *identify anomalies,* gain an understanding of them, communicate the new knowledge to clients, and incorporate the findings into practical tools.

As previously noted, the research tools help to continually pinpoint situations where there is a patterned mismatch between actual stock prices and the warranted prices calculated with the existing algorithms for implementing the life-cycle valuation model. This often leads to learning how to better adjust accounting data to approximate economic returns. This in turn leads to improved discount rates and a sharper lens by which to identify new anomalies, perhaps concerning investor expectations. With this intensive, looped working with data within the context of a specified valuation model, every so often, a fundamental breakthrough would occur, such as a superior way to forecast long-term fade rates. Knowledge building (Gilbert and Christensen, 2005) through a systematic identification and study of anomalies (large differences between warranted versus actual stock prices) holds much promise for finance researchers.[11]

Anomalies offer a fruitful path to improve the valuation model itself, or more likely, the calculation of input variables to the model. In terms of the PAK Loop, one begins with a purpose of evaluating and improving a particular valuation model. Anomalies are perceptions that cause problems for the existing knowledge base or model. This leads to a more penetrating analysis of cause and effect that, if successful, yields a change (action) that improves the tracking of warranted versus actual stock prices (consequence). In general, the testing and evaluation of alternative hypotheses provides critically important feedback that would not have occurred if the anomalies were treated as regression equation outliers and ignored.

INVESTOR EXPECTATIONS: THE WAL-MART EXAMPLE

Mainstream finance, as reflected in corporate finance textbooks, has little to say about how the users of valuation models can develop skill in making forecasts. In other words, the users' forecasting skill is viewed as being independent from the model. Not so with the life-cycle research program. The three primary research tools—life-cycle track records, valuation model, and warranted value charts—comprise the product provided to institutional money manager clients, who sharpen their forecasting skills by participating in the same learning process as the research staff.

When users employ these tools to investigate a firm, they gain an opportunity to study the causes of a firm's long-term fade within the unique context of an industry and economic environment, and to build up expertise in understanding how "the market" makes long-term forecasts (sets expectations) and revises these expectations as new data arrive.

The more experience users have with these tools, the better prepared they are to analyze a company. There are two main analytical benefits. First, users gain insights as to the key valuation issues for a particular firm and to potential management strategies to most favorably impact shareholder value. Second, the users' growing base of experience facilitates plausibility judgments about investor forecasts (expectations), their own forecasts, and the forecasts of others. Judging the degree of difficulty in achieving these forecasted levels of performance is greatly aided by comparison to the type of companies that historically achieved these same levels of life-cycle performance.

As for plausibility judgments and investor expectations, an informative application of the life-cycle model was reported in a September 9, 1996, *Forbes* article, "Follow the Cash: HOLT Value Associates Hated Wal-Mart in 1991; Its Unique Valuation System Tells HOLT to Love Wal-Mart Now" (Samuels, 1996). The article described the life-cycle framework used by HOLT in consulting with institutional investors. *Forbes* pointed out that HOLT had rated Wal-Mart as a strong sell five years earlier before it sharply declined, whereas HOLT now considered Wal-Mart a strong buy. The main point is not that these two recommendations produced returns consistent with the sell/buy recommendations; rather, the important point is the judgment process for competitive fade and managerial skill at those two points in time versus investor expectations.

Although the Wal-Mart success story is well known, the magnitude of Wal-Mart's wealth-creation achievement is striking when displayed in life-cycle terms as seen in Figure 5.4. CFROI returns rose from 12 to about 15 percent from 1970 to 1990, coupled with enormous real asset growth rates. That remarkable performance was continually underestimated by investors and the stock outperformed the S&P 500 by 100-fold over that 20-year span.

In 1991, Wal-Mart's stock price implied no downward competitive fade in both CFROI returns and real asset growth rates for the next five years. While possible, our experience suggested that at its much bigger size relative to the 1970s and 1980s, Wal-Mart was unlikely to meet those extremely optimistic investor expectations. The stock subsequently underperformed the market substantially from 1991 to 1996 (see bottom panel of Figure 5.4) as CFROI returns declined and asset growth sharply fell off.

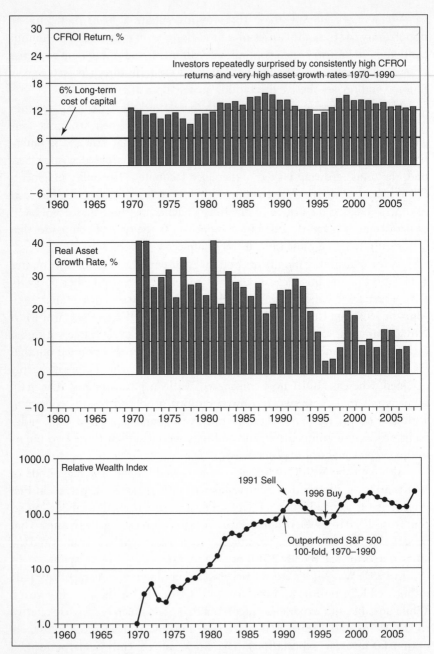

FIGURE 5.4 Wal-Mart
Source: Credit Suisse HOLT ValueSearch® global database.

At the time of the 1996 *Forbes* article, investor expectations were for Wal-Mart's CFROI returns to rapidly fade downward over the next five years to a level close to the long-term corporate average of 6 percent CFROI returns. We felt comfortable in betting against an expectation that Wal-Mart was on the verge of becoming an average firm. This time, the stock subsequently rose sharply more than the S&P 500 during the next three years as Wal-Mart handily beat the 1996 expectations.

Although it is convenient to distill investor expectations into a single, best-estimate forecast, more rigorous analysis deals with warranted value as the expected value of a probability-weighted distribution of scenarios for future fade of economic returns and reinvestment rates (Alessandri, Ford, Lander, Leggio, and Taylor, 2004). Real options analysis is relevant for dealing with alternative scenarios, although application at the firm level is substantially more difficult compared to the project level.

To illustrate the concept of fade distribution, let's return to Figure 5.4 and reflect on the process that produced such extraordinary excess shareholder returns during the 1970s and 1980s. At various times during this period, I analyzed Wal-Mart and decided not to buy it because I viewed the probability as low for a scenario in which Wal-Mart would maintain high CFROI returns while sustaining an extraordinarily high 25-percent-per-year organic asset growth rate. I was wrong. My mistake was in not sufficiently understanding Wal-Mart's business model and exceptional managerial skill, which enabled the firm to perform so spectacularly as to drive its chief competitor, Kmart, into bankruptcy on its way to becoming the dominant retail company in the United States.

CRITICAL ACCOUNTING ISSUES

Financial statements should be constructed to be useful to investors. In striving for usefulness, there are two especially troublesome issues that currently concern accounting rule-makers: fair value for balance sheet items and intangible assets.

There is a widespread perception that, on logical grounds, no one should argue against expressing balance sheet items in terms of their current value instead of their historical cost value (CFA Institute, 2005; Miller and Bahnson, 2007). Proponents of fair value accounting assume that a point-in-time (balance sheet) measure of an asset that more closely approximates market value is unquestionably more useful for investors. Let's take a closer look at that assumption.

The previous discussion on valuation stressed the role of economic returns, track records, and managerial skill as critical to investors in forecasting a firm's long-term, net cash receipt stream. In particular, an economic return, being an achieved return, expresses what was received weighed against what was given up. In turn, the comparison of economic returns to a firm's cost of capital can be used as a gauge of managerial skill.

An economic return cannot be measured if the original (historical) cost outlays are unavailable. Clearly, this argues for requiring the reporting of historical cost figures. But supplementary information on estimated market values for balance sheet items can certainly be helpful. For example, scrutiny of a firm's existing assets should, as noted earlier, include analysis of the potential value of assets to others who may be better able to use buildings, land, and the like.

As for intangibles, it is widely agreed that this is an especially difficult and important challenge (Corrado, Haltiwanger, and Sichel, 2005; Hand and Lev, 2003). The conceptual accounting issue is invariably framed around the definition of an asset. Outlays for R&D, employee training, advertising, organizational changes to improve processes, and the like can certainly generate benefits well beyond the current accounting period, which argues for capitalization as assets.[12] But the issue is not so simple.

Accounting rule makers view the intangibles issue through a conceptual lens that serves up the following difficulties:

- Decide which outlays clearly will bring benefits in future years and should be treated as "investments" and recorded as assets on the balance sheet so that future revenues will be matched with appropriate expenses.
- Quantify the amortization schedules that reflect how the intangible assets will depreciate in the future.

This way of framing the problem assumes that a solution necessarily involves crafting new accounting standards for capitalization and amortization of intangibles. This is because accounting rule makers are guided by a fundamental principle that revenues need to be matched to expenses to make accounting earnings useful. With this way of thinking, the rule makers must figure out an answer to each type of intangible and then translate these beliefs into accounting standards.

Let's frame the problem differently and focus on the valuation needs of investors and the notion that the more valuable the intangible outlay, the harder to quantify for accounting purposes. For example, outlays that enhance a firm's knowledge-creation capability are especially instrumental in a firm gaining competitive advantage:

> Unlike physical assets, knowledge assets are process rather than substance, and therefore in continuous change. They are an indispensable, internal resource for creating values that cannot be readily bought and sold. Much of a firm's economic value is measured in explicit knowledge assets, such as know-how, patents, copyrights, and brand image, because they are easier to measure. But, in fact, these are the results of past knowledge-creation endeavors. The more valuable asset is the underlying tacit knowledge that was needed to create them because that knowledge and its methodology are the source of knowledge-creation capability at the firm and therefore the gauge of future value.
>
> (Nonaka, Toyama, and Hirata, 2008, p. 42)

One approach to intangibles is for accounting information to include relevant details about intangible outlays so that investors could use this information in whatever ways are most workable for their valuation models. At any point in time, some investors might choose not to attempt to capitalize and amortize a particular intangible item, and instead adjust their long-term fade forecast for economic returns as a way to capture the impact of this intangible investment. Perhaps many investors would be comfortable with the capitalization and amortization of R&D expenditures as required by new accounting rules. Perhaps some investors with especially deep knowledge about certain industries would want to handle R&D differently.

This approach puts a premium on flexibility and learning and is conducive to a new accounting system evolving over time. Investors, provided with detailed information, would have choices in how to handle intangibles. Consumer choice and competition can work even for accounting standards.

The above is not an abstract idea; rather it is eminently practical due to the emergence of XBRL—Extensible Business Reporting Language (www.xbrl.org). With XBRL, accounting items are tagged with precise definitions enabling fine-grained analysis as opposed to aggregate accounting data (e.g., a net plant figure). With electronic access to company financial statement data, investors would be able to manipulate XBRL information about intangibles according to the needs of their own valuation models.

REPLY TO CRITICS

Those who have written books on valuation obviously have strong beliefs that their approach to the topic has considerable merit. In defending their recommended approach, some authors of these books have been especially critical of two concepts of the life-cycle valuation model: first, company-specific, market-derived discount rates, and second, measurement in units of constant purchasing power (real). In my opinion, the underlying reasons for their criticisms are the lack of a systems mindset and an aversion to the type of research and analysis required if the above two concepts were accepted.

The lack of a systems mindset is apparent in Bennett Stewart's (1994, p. 83) rejection of market-derived discount rates: ". . . rather than using a risk-adjusted cost of capital as computed from the Capital Asset Pricing Model or Arbitrage Pricing model, as academic theory recommends, . . . HOLT *solves* for the cost of capital . . . given the forecasts they project. This is circular reasoning . . . it makes the cost of capital depend upon the specific forecasting method they choose to employ." Also lacking a systems mind-set are Erik Stern and Mike Hutchinson (2004, p. 51), who note: "CFROI subjectively and arbitrarily 'calculates' the cost of capital by discounting investment analysts' forecasts of a company's performance."

Tom Copeland (2005) seems uninterested in the comparison of a firm's long-term time series of estimated economic returns (estimated from reported financial statements) versus a benchmark cost of capital, which I argue demands the use of real measurement units. Further, Copeland (2005, p. 297) says: "Frankly, it is a mystery to us why one would use the same GDP deflator for all types of plant and equipment—let's say a computer system and a 20-megawatt generator." With clear thinking about an economic return there is no mystery.

The *achieved* return on investment for a completed project—the economic return—indicates to investors how well the project has done. It is eminently sensible to express this performance in terms of monetary units of constant purchasing power and that requires all cash outflows and inflows to be adjusted for changes in the purchasing power of the dollar via the GDP deflator, or some other broad index of price changes. The type of equipment used in the project is not relevant to investors. The achieved real ROI matters.

Consider management undertaking a project with a one-year life. The project begins with the purchase of a machine for $100 having a one-year life. Cash flow of $200 is received at year end. Although there is zero inflation as reflected in the general price level as measured by the GDP deflator, the cost to replace the machine at year-end is $200. Are investors pleased?

The achieved (economic) return is a real 100 percent—that is, spend $100 and receive $200 one year later. Investors should be quite happy. But an accountant with an eye for "inflation adjustments" announces that investors should be quite unhappy. Depreciation charges adjusted for the doubling of replacement cost would be $200 and this would consume the $200 of cash flow.

This simple example reveals the importance of clear thinking not only about an economic return, but also about the previously discussed way of thinking about existing assets. First, without any ambiguity, investors are clearly rewarded with an achieved real return of 100 percent. Second, whether the machine is replaced is a separate issue involving an investment decision by management.

The notion of automatically reinvesting depreciation charges to maintain the "going concern" confuses the difference between existing assets whose cash flows wind down over their useful lives and new investments that need their own economic justification. Confusion on this matter was at the heart of the SEC's fiasco in the 1970s to require U.S. companies to report replacement costs.

I conclude this chapter with an observation reflecting my long involvement with the life-cycle approach. "Believers" in either CAPM, EVA, life-cycle model, or whatever new model attracts their attention can easily lose skepticism about what they think they know. Opportunity to improve one's knowledge base is lost due to complacency. Theory building often makes the most progress when problems are approached from new angles, where a healthy competition exists among alternative models, and commitment is strong to actively search for situations where one's preferred model does poorly or fails (Madden, 2009a).

Valuation models and related data displays should be judged according to their usefulness to analysts and investors for gaining insights from analyzing firms' histories, identifying and communicating key valuation issues, quantifying investor expectations, and assisting in making plausibility judgments about forecasts. In addition, they should be judged in terms of the results achieved from the users' buy/hold/sell decisions. Tradeoff decisions involving simplicity versus complexity suggest that no one approach best fits all environments.

All existing models face a serious challenge in dealing with companies that have very high levels of intangibles. For such companies, future research might lead to radically different ways to handle the fundamental task of forecasting a firm's long-term, net cash receipt stream.

Summary of Key Ideas

- In the life-cycle framework, a firm's level of economic returns, relative to its cost of capital, and its reinvestment rate are the key quantitative measures that reflect wealth creation or dissipation. Track record displays of these variables answer the question of how to measure management's long-term performance.

- Management should quantify their business units' performance as life-cycle track records and then base reinvestment decisions on the following wealth-creation principle: Investors will value the firm's reinvestment outlays that are expected to achieve economic returns that exceed/equal/fall below the opportunity cost of capital at market prices that exceed/equal/fall below the cost basis for those outlays.

- On one hand, all else equal, a *higher* reinvestment rate in business units earning returns above the cost of capital creates more wealth. On the other hand, all else equal, a *longer* time period for sustaining economic returns above the cost of capital (favorable fade) creates more wealth. All else is never equal, especially since higher reinvestment rates tend to be associated with faster downward fade of wealth-creating economic returns. As such, management's strategy for expansion should strive to achieve the *optimum* blend of future fade rates for economic returns and reinvestment rates.

- When a valuation model and the inputs it uses have given top priority to mathematical elegance or measurement convenience, this can easily lead to lost opportunities for revealing insights that can lead to better decisions. A prime example is the approximation for the value of existing assets. Another example is the use of unadjusted accounting ROIs such as RONA.

- The life-cycle valuation model along with its related track records and warranted value charts can serve as a uniquely useful learning system. As users gain experience with these tools, they become better equipped to make plausibility judgments about forecasts of firm performance, including market expectations implied in current stock prices. They become more astute in analyzing the impact on shareholder value of a firm's existing strategy versus alternative strategies.

- With the life-cycle research program, valuation anomalies are not ignored as outliers. Rather, anomalies are welcomed since they are the source for improved understanding and increased accuracy.

- Any discounted cash flow valuation model is a system of interrelated components, or variables. Therefore, the estimate of a discount rate to be used in a specific model should be tied to the way that net cash receipts are forecasted. This is particularly relevant to models incorporating standard ways of forecasting future fade rates based on company characteristics.

- Although not easy to calculate, forward-looking, market-derived discount rates, as employed in the life-cycle model, overcome some significant problems with CAPM/Beta-derived discount rates.

- With a systems mindset, "risk adjustment" can be made either in terms of a higher/lower discount rate or with a less/more favorable fade forecast. The benefit of the latter is that investors gain a better intuitive understanding of the adjustment being made.

- The life-cycle research experience shows that information most needed for valuation purposes varies according to valuation frameworks and their stages of development. With the accelerated implementation of XBRL, fine-grained data (on intangibles, for instance) could be made available to investors, and many would experiment with this information to learn how to better analyze companies. In time, this process would reveal what information is most important much better than any rule-making bodies could possibly decide.

CHAPTER 6

Business Firms as Lean, Value-Added Systems

Lean is not a manufacturing tactic. Lean is not a cost-reduction program. Lean is a business strategy. The reason for focusing most of the initial attention on manufacturing processes is that is where most of the value-added activities that need to be liberated take place. Cost savings are achieved over time, but that takes place in the context of implementing lean as a business strategy. . . . [S]uccessfully implementing a lean strategy requires that people change the culture of their companies so that they think and behave lean. . . .

The key to changing values and beliefs, and thereby culture, is to require people to behave differently so that they can experience a set of results that are better than what they have experienced in the past. As this happens over and over again, they evolve to a new set of values and beliefs (thinking lean) that drives new behaviors (acting lean) yielding better results (being lean).

—Orest Fiume, *Lean Accounting: Best Practices for Sustainable Integration*

The superior performance of lean companies, such as Toyota and Danaher, is widely recognized and studied. Nevertheless, it has proven very difficult for companies to make a lean transformation and to sustain the continuous improvement that is the hallmark of lean operations. This chapter is devoted to a deeper understanding of business firms as lean, value-added systems.

Recall how, in Chapter 1, we developed the PAK Loop framework for handling the getting-smarter, or knowledge-base-building, process. Now combine the PAK Loop with lean thinking. The following overview of lean principles is organized by components of the PAK Loop, beginning with the knowledge base. The overview also builds on the lean narratives in the book, *Lean Thinking: Banish Waste and Create Wealth in Your Corporation* (Womack and Jones, 2003).

LEAN THINKING AND PAK LOOP COMPONENTS

Business firms are complex systems. A systems mindset is needed to effectively deal with an evolving, complex system. To guide management in improving firm performance, system principles are needed that have already proven useful in a wide range of industries. James Womack and Daniel Jones fill this need with their superb research program (Womack, Jones, and Ross, 1990; Womack and Jones, 2003, 2005) on lean thinking/management (their websites are www.lean.org and www.leanuk.org).

These researchers have condensed lean thinking, as pioneered by Toyota, into five core principles, "... precisely specify *value* by specific product, identify the *value stream* for each product, make value *flow* without interruptions, let the customer *pull* value from the producer, and pursue *perfection*" (James P. Womack and Daniel T. Jones, 2003, p. 10, italics in original).

The transformation of a business to lean thinking depends on much more than the implementation of some of Toyota's best practices. A lean transformation requires a commitment, at every level of a firm, to a culture of continuously getting smarter in eliminating *muda* (the Japanese word for waste) while, at the same time, providing ever more value to customers.

In the following sections, I discuss implementation details of the five core lean principles. These details make more sense when put into the context of a PAK Loop for building knowledge at a rapid rate, which is the underlying source of sustained competitive advantage.

Knowledge Base

In Chapter 1, high-reliability organizations, such as aircraft carriers and firefighting crews, were shown to adhere to a culture of mindfulness. People in these organizations excel in managing the unexpected because they rapidly improve their knowledge base and therefore make better, faster decisions.

What distinguishes the Toyota culture, which enables the company to rapidly and continuously improve its processes for delivering value to customers? Steven Spear and H. Kent Bowen persuasively argue that Toyota's culture simultaneously combines an extraordinary focus on the standardization of work with flexibility in solving problems:

> [Y]ou have to see that the rigid specification is the very thing that makes the flexibility and creativity possible. . . . [T]he key is to understand that the Toyota Production System creates a community of scientists. Whenever Toyota delivers a specification, it is establishing sets of hypotheses that can be tested. In other words, it is following the scientific method. . . . The fact that the scientific method is so ingrained at Toyota explains why the high degree of specification and structure at the company does not promote the command and control environment one might expect. Indeed, in watching people doing their jobs and in helping to design production processes, we learned that the system actually stimulates workers and managers to engage in the kind of experimentation that is widely recognized as the cornerstone of a learning organization. That is what distinguishes Toyota from all the other companies we studied.
>
> (Spear and Bowen, 1999)

To nurture such a culture requires upper levels of management to have a deep knowledge and commitment to the five core principles of lean thinking. Conversely, the conventional corporate hierarchy of command and control of employees is at cross-purposes with a culture rooted in lean thinking. A hierarchical control process is typically tied to "making the accounting numbers." That motivates the kind of short-term behavior that is not attuned to long-term improvement. The control language that permeates this type of outmoded organization is often based on the assumption that lower costs are achieved through higher production volume.

Consequently, one may be skeptical of a self-proclaimed "lean" company whose management does not actually practice lean as a way of life, but simply uses some of the lean tools to improve workflow or reduce inventories while still using standard accounting numbers as the actual incentive to control people. Incentives need to promote teamwork to solve problems at their source as part of a system geared to eliminate waste and to deliver defect-free products. Tom Johnson aptly summarizes the fork-in-the-road for top management:

> No company that talks about improving performance can know what it is doing if its primary window on results is financial information and not system principles. No amount of financial manipulation will ever improve long-term results. Performance in the long run will improve only if managers ensure that the system from which the performance emerges adheres more and more closely to principles resembling those that guide the operations of a living system. The dilemma facing all companies that intend to become "lean" is that they can follow a truly systemic path to lean or they can continue to use management accounting "levers of control." They can't do both.
>
> (Johnson, 2007, p. 13)

Accounting-based performance measures are driven by the profitability of *existing* assets on the balance sheet. One can observe, across companies in all stages of their life cycles, a strong motivation for management to efficiently use existing assets and core competencies. Further, management compensation is often structured in ways that most reward efficiency gains from existing resources. The end result is the prevalent *assumption* that figuring out the best way to use existing resources is the same as understanding best value for customers. That way of thinking can easily block feedback from recognizing possible big jumps in value to customers from novel ideas involving resources or skills not part of the firm's existing assets.

We have now returned to the critical issue of understanding why it is so difficult for firms to continually "beat the fade" and sustain superior levels of economic performance (Beinhocker, 2006). A firm's culture reflects embedded ways of doing things that worked (not unlike an individual's knowledge base). On one hand, changing the business model could better position the firm for a future environment that is much different than the past. On the other hand, this could disrupt the existing organization and depress today's profits while bringing uncertainty about future profits. How should management deal with this often paralyzing dilemma?

The answer is to follow lean thinking's core principle of extraordinary focus on the specification of *value* to the customer. This means being flexible when evolving a business model for a product, or family of products, based on learning how to optimize value to the customer. A focus on the customer reduces the risk of doing things in a new way and investing in different assets and capabilities. Ignoring this principle can result in higher prices, over time, for products or services that provide features of little value to customers. At some point, competitors will exploit that kind of situation and the comfort of business as usual will quickly vanish.

Eastman Kodak's competitive decline was marked by slow adaptation to changing consumer needs coupled with high manufacturing costs (low profits) for new products. Also, Kodak's culture was one of exceptional control of every aspect of its business. At one point, Kodak even manufactured its own cardboard containers in which to package its products. In sharp contrast, Apple's iPod was a beautifully integrated solution that optimized value to the customer. Apple outsourced many of the manufacturing activities and achieved high profitability.

Purposes

When asked what their goals or purposes are, managements are most likely to respond, "Value to the customer, productivity, and shareholder value." Their perceptions of problems, actions taken, and feedback received more or less revolve around these key elements. However, background relevant to their response is not often critically examined. Namely, the fundamental way that work is organized and that information flows in the firm tends to be accepted automatically.

Yet the experiences of lean companies indicate that the most critical part of delivering value to the customer and of eliminating waste is to organize work as a steady system of continuous *flow*, in effect, making products one at a time to meet demand. Optimizing flow through a system of components of the right size, right fit, and right design (Huntzinger, 2007, p. 21) will reduce inventories, storage areas, reworking, capital costs for high-capacity machines, and especially wasted time.

Firms organized for mass production, whether manufacturers or service businesses, seek economy of scale with large batches that require substantial buffers, such as work-in-process inventories and allowances for time delays. They are not organized to make the entire system flow to achieve overall efficiency, but to optimize local efficiencies. Information systems for mass-production firms tend to be based on the standard cost accounting system, which motivates employees to achieve the lowest unit cost per product through long production runs that absorb overhead.

Buffers, such as large inventories, hide problems. Conversely, in a one-piece flow system, problems quickly surface. Consequently, problems demand immediate attention. Early and immediate action builds quality into the process itself. With lean flow and a Toyota-style respect for employees' abilities to solve problems, employees at every step of production are also acting as quality inspectors. Toyota's respect for employees is similar in spirit and results to Nucor's genuine empowerment of its steelworkers to improve productivity.

Firms that continually improve lean processes free up resources and *create unused capacity* that can be employed to support additional sales growth. This is monumentally important for generating long-term wealth for shareholders. Recall that the value of the firm is the present value of its long-term, net cash receipt stream. Also recall that net cash receipts are cash coming into a firm, less cash paid out for new capacity and related investments. Consequently, the lean bottom line is bigger net cash receipts over the long haul. Finally, when additional capacity is needed, it can be added in *small increments* that entail little risk because the additions are attuned to actual customer demand rather than forecasted demand.

We are now touching on the basic point made by Orest Fiume in the quotation at the beginning of this chapter. *Lean is a business strategy.* Sustaining the five core lean principles equips a firm to exploit opportunities. In addition to freeing up resources to fund growth initiatives, lean delivers a lower cost structure as well as the flexibility to make a wide range of products. That in turn widens the menu of strategic choices. Moreover, novel approaches to the design of products and services can result from systems thinking focused on every detail of the customer experience with a product or service (Womack and Jones, 2005).

Systems thinking is needed to improve the work processes that generate long-term shareholder value. A serious roadblock occurs when CEOs and boards of directors believe that the key to shareholder value is to meet or exceed Wall Street's quarterly earnings expectations. This can easily lead to a lack of meaningful progress in improving value-added processes and a resulting fast competitive fade—similar to Kmart's experience prior to its bankruptcy.

In my opinion, the ideal solution is for top management and the board to adopt a wealth-creation framework that connects *long-term* financial results both to shareholder value and to the core lean activities that generate financial results. This solution is described in Chapter 7 and has the desirable effect of enabling top management to stop dancing to Wall Street's quarterly earnings tune while at the same time making better decisions for the benefit of long-term shareholders.

Perceptions

Using a systems view, *value streams* need to be developed that encompass the entire production process of a product, culminating with the end customer. Managers must think beyond the confines of their firm to include maps of process details of upstream suppliers, downstream distributors, and the like anywhere in the stream. Purge waste everywhere.

Womack and Jones described a value stream project undertaken by Pratt & Whitney, which is a large manufacturer of jet engines and a division of United Technologies:

> . . . [Pratt & Whitney] . . . discovered that activities undertaken by its raw materials suppliers to produce ultrapure metals were duplicated at great cost by the next firms downstream, the forgers who converted metal ingots into near-net shapes suitable for machining. At the same time, the initial ingot of material—for example, titanium or nickel—was ten times the weight of the machined parts eventually fashioned from it. Ninety percent of the very expensive metals were being scrapped because the initial ingot was poured in a massive size—the melters were certain that this was efficient—without much attention to the shape of the finished parts. And finally, the melters were preparing several different ingots—at great cost—in order to meet Pratt's precise technical requirements for each engine, which varied only marginally from those of other engine families and from the needs of competitors. Many of these activities could be eliminated almost immediately with dramatic cost savings.
>
> (Womack and Jones, 2003, p. 20)

Prior to this analysis of the entire value stream, neither Pratt & Whitney nor its suppliers perceived massive waste. *Perceptions depend on one's way of thinking.*

A careful study of every activity required to deliver a final product is the key to an initial assessment of waste—that is, activity that adds no value but is currently an integral part of the workflow. Womack and Jones indicated that a typical walk along a non-lean firm's value stream shows that 80 to 90 percent of the total steps are waste from the standpoint of customer value, and 99 percent of throughput time is waste.

Keep in mind that how one perceives inefficiency/waste can be quite different when value stream mapping has replaced a conventional cost accounting perspective. In fact, certain components of the value stream may use expensive and high-output machines to optimize local accounting-based efficiencies only to be the root cause of waste farther downstream in transportations costs, storage costs, and time delays.

Whether for value stream mapping or specific problem solving, Toyota is adamant about *gemba*—that is, go see for yourself in order to accurately perceive a problem situation. This is diametrically opposite to a command-and-control hierarchy that relies on memos and reports to inform upper levels of management.

Cause and Effect

In a typical batch manufacturing firm, large finished-goods inventory gets pushed to end customers. The internal scheduling required in a push system will magnify the variability in customer demand to the detriment of a stable system.

A transition from a push to a *pull* work environment enables employees to work smarter by applying a scientifically sound process to improve work processes. Whether applied to a manufacturing or service business, the basic idea of pull is that an upstream activity ideally produces a good or service only when the next downstream activity requests it.

A successful pull implementation will typically lead to a decline in inventories and cycle time, smoother production flow, and higher quality with lower cost (Hopp and Spearman, 2004, p. 137). This in turn will bring to the surface all sorts of problems that are hidden within a push environment and its concomitant greater work-in-process. Having problems surface is a prerequisite to understanding cause and effect in order to solve these problems.

Pull is one of many important lean tools. But, in a desire to be known as a lean company, managements all too often have installed Toyota tools without appreciating the importance of building from a foundation of problem-solving employees—that is, employees who have been and will be continuously coached and mentored by skilled, lean managers. Managements can be easily enamored with tools to the detriment of fully applying the total system approach. Lean tools are not the desired goal. A targeted business result is the goal.

Consider *kanbans*, which are signaling devices used by Toyota for either the production or withdrawal of items in a pull system. Lots of kanbans are a sign of a lean company, right? Such thinking misses the fundamental point that in an *ideal* production system there would be no need for kanbans.

In terms of popular choice, along with the use of kanbans are *kaizen* workshops in which a team implements a significant process improvement, usually over a five-day period. More kaizens equals more lean, right? Again, let's focus on business results. A particular kaizen may succeed in raising throughput in a production cell, but it may not translate into increased throughput for the overall system. Why? Because the activity chosen for a kaizen was not a bottleneck (key constraint) in the first place.

A last example is inventory, which everyone *knows* should be radically reduced in order to achieve lean-type efficiency. Wrong. Any ironclad rule, or absolute statement, is inconsistent with a systems mindset. In that regard, I once heard a noted lean expert, with an exceptional long-term track record in delivering business results, describe a major improvement to a plant that was part of his division. This plant had a huge seasonal demand that created all sorts of problems. His solution was to *increase inventories*, which enabled the leveling out of production throughout the year and produced higher profits with greatly reduced stress for employees.

Actions and Consequences

The kind of sustained improvement achieved by Toyota remains elusive for most firms that begin by simply applying some lean tools. There are at least two explanations for this failure to make significant progress.

First, an analysis followed by implementation may be executed by consultants or management without ownership by the front-line employees. Some improvement will be achieved if a grossly inefficient work process is improved. But this efficiency gain can easily plateau or regress if front-line employees were not the primary focus. Also, implementation of lean tools often brings problems to the surface. To solve these problems as a normal part of the work environment requires highly motivated and adequately trained front-line employees that are enthusiastically supported by managers.

The key point here is that management should focus on people first, then target a business result, and then implement the change best suited to deliver the desired business result. These changes will most likely involve lean tools, but the tools are a means to a desired end and not the end itself.

The second explanation addresses Tom Johnson's point about the *management system bottleneck* that fundamentally makes a lean transformation, yielding sustained improvement, so difficult to achieve. Sustained improvement, targeted at the elimination of all waste in order to deliver high value to customers, is the essence of the fifth lean principle—*perfection*. The quest for perfection requires a very special culture that must be guided and mentored by top management.

For CEOs (and boards of directors) to truly assert, "Employees are our most important asset" and "Efficiently delivering value to the customer is our purpose," necessitates a management system and culture that reflects lean system principles. Yet most managements control their organizations through accounting-based and end-of-period data from various departments. Instead of this vertical control orientation, the focus should be on improving, in real time, value streams that run horizontally across the firm. The focus of work, whether by front-line employees, departmental staff, or management, must be on continuously improving the processes that make up the value streams. It is a mistake to attempt to control the results instead of organizing work to improve the processes that produce the results (Johnson and Bröms, 2000).

Feedback

Once management adopts a lean systems mindset, functions and departments within the firm are viewed as being supportive of value streams. This has profound implications for the kinds of feedback that are needed in a lean organization.

When work is standardized, abnormalities are immediately observed. Managers need to work with employees in the role of knowledgeable coaches who help employees get to the root causes of problems. This type of feedback not only promotes more problem identification and solution, it also promotes a sense among employees that they *own* that part of a process for which they have responsibility. Further, employees continuously get smarter as a natural result of doing their jobs.

In contrast, the worst kind of command-and-control hierarchy reacts negatively to problems, and circumvents employee involvement by having supervisors "fix" problems that arise. This typically results in poor morale on the part of employees and in firefighting and working around what is actually a systemic problem instead of dealing with a solution that addresses the root cause of the problem.

As for root causes, an informative contrast between Toyota and a command-and-control hierarchy is evident in Toyota's A3 report. An *A3 report* refers to a standard 11-by-17-inch sheet of paper. An A3 report allows for one page only, and is organized in sections corresponding to the four needs of Deming's *PDCA cycle*. The *Plan–Do–Check–Act* learning cycle is Toyota's application of the scientific method: hypothesis–try–reflect–adjust. The importance of PDCA to the Toyota culture cannot be overstated. It is used at all levels of the firm as a way of thinking and communicating.

A3s are typically crafted by employees undertaking an important change within a process. The A3 author uses the document to engage in a dialogue with those affected by the proposed change. Feedback from those employees brings to the surface disagreements and generates new ideas. After laying out the entire thinking process as a one-page proposal, and receiving feedback from those closest to the situation, the final version of an A3 is supposed to reflect agreement on a scientifically sound plan for improvement. Moreover, A3s enable managers to mentor employees through Socratic-style discussions geared to solving problems and promoting learning. This kind of mentoring takes place within the context of an employee taking full responsibility for getting the decision made and implemented. John Shook summarizes the role of A3s in a lean organization as follows:

> [T]he most important function of the proposal A3 is to provide a mechanism for companies to authorize activities, while keeping the initiation of the action in the hands of the person doing the work, the responsible individual. . . . In factories, responsibility is usually clear, especially for production workers. The challenge is getting people to think. In offices or other forms of knowledge work, where everyone's job is to think, the problem is that responsibility is often muddled. . . . The underlying way of thinking reframes all activities as learning activities at every level of the organization, whether it's standardized work and kaizen at the micro/individual level, system kaizen at the managerial level, or major strategic/tactical decisions at the corporate level . . . based on 1) understanding causality, 2) seeking predictability, and 3) ensuring ongoing, unending learning.
>
> (Shook, 2008, p. 120)

A fair conclusion is that Toyota's replacing the traditional corporate memos with A3s represents a serious commitment to the Toyota way of doing things that bears repetition—understanding causality, seeking predictability, and ensuring learning.

A LEAN TRANSFORMATION EXAMPLE: DANAHER

In the early 1980s, Steven and Mitchell Rales took over a poorly performing company (a former real estate investment trust) and began making acquisitions. Thus began the building of Danaher Corporation, which is widely acknowledged today as the preeminent U.S. lean company.

The Rales brothers were financial dealmakers, not manufacturing experts. One of their early acquisitions was Jake Brake, which pioneered lean manufacturing in the United States. The Rales brothers paid a great deal of attention to the superb performance of Jake Brake. With top management pushing lean as the top priority, all of Danaher's business units implemented lean principles. Many of their units were in unglamorous businesses such as industrial tools. But their operating performance became stellar.

Danaher has remained a highly acquisitive company and has developed expertise in quickly applying its Danaher Business System (DBS) to acquired firms, which then quickly produce exceptional gains in performance. DBS is Danaher's lean way of thinking for exceeding customer expectations as defined by quality, delivery, cost, and innovation. DBS has evolved from application to manufacturing to encompass all of the firm's functions, including R&D.

Mark DeLuzio, an early leader in lean implementation, and a key architect of the Danaher Business System, commented as follows on the changes to the culture at Danaher:

> The top guys have to be totally committed to it [lean]. They have to become educated and when I say educated I mean benchmarking like you wouldn't believe: going to Japan, seeing the best companies, talking to people who are doing it . . . . They also have to become educated not only from a book sense but a hands-on sense in terms of participating because the light bulbs don't turn on until you actually do it. It's not until the light bulbs go on and they truly internalize it that they will start creating a culture. . . . At the end of the day people do what the boss is expecting them to do. . . . They have to be measured on quality, delivery and how they solve problems. . . . A lot of managers today are only being measured on results and they are not being measured on creating the business process. . . . The whole measurement system and how we measure people on results is our biggest problem. The senior guys have to understand that. They have to be asking for the sustainable

business process that gets the result as well as the result itself. That is the culture shift that has to happen. Without that happening at the very top level, it's not going to take over.

(DeLuzio, 2001, p. 8)

Figure 6.1 shows that Danaher's shareholders have been rewarded since 1982 with a remarkable trend in outperforming the S&P 500.

Danaher illustrates the point that top management and the board should seek to develop their own way of implementing the five core lean principles. On one hand, Danaher demonstrates high "conventional" lean skills and the generation of substantial cash flows to fund new investments. On the other hand, Danaher management has widely implemented its customized DBS so that all employees know how their daily search for improvements in handling their jobs connects to the firm's goals. Such employee alignment and motivation is quite difficult to accomplish. In addition, Danaher management is very skilled in making acquisitions that achieve high economic returns based on the price paid for the acquisition. The firm's portfolio of businesses has evolved to include higher technology businesses that fit carefully planned, strategic platforms.

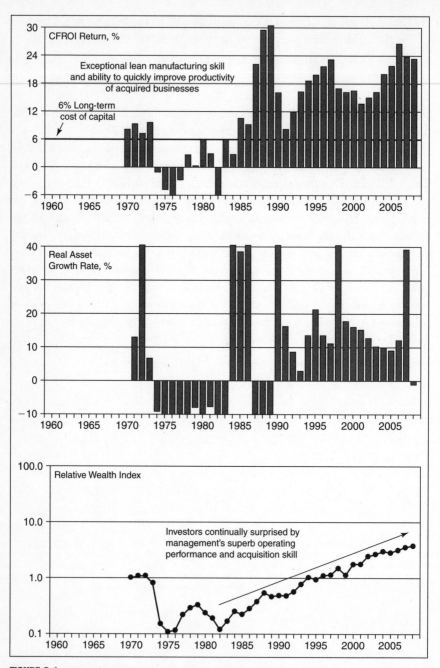

FIGURE 6.1 Danaher
Source: Credit Suisse HOLT ValueSearch® global database.

Summary of Key Ideas

- A successful lean company transformation, à la Danaher, will create substantial wealth for the long-term benefit of customers, employees, and shareholders. This observable result supports the private-sector initiative, introduced at the end of Chapter 3, which recommends accelerating lean implementation in order to promote economic prosperity.

- Systems thinking is a hand-in-glove fit with lean thinking. A focus on each product's, or family of products', value stream leads to a systems view that extends beyond the confines of the firm. Purge activities, wherever located, that do not add value to the end customers. Avoid a tunnel focus on local, accounting-based efficiencies and continually improve processes that optimize the overall system.

- A lean firm organizes work processes in a continuous flow in which an upstream activity produces a good or service only when the next downstream activity requests it. Such an organization surfaces problems that would be hidden in a large batch process with buffers such as big inventories. Buffers hide problems. Lean companies recognize and solve problems at their source.

- The absence of a systems mindset typically accounts for top management's implementing one or more lean tools, but within a hierarchical management structure that emphasizes vertical control keyed to accounting cost data. Missing is a top-to-bottom culture that gives front-line employees responsibility and support to continually solve problems. In contrast, successful lean companies have a problem-solving culture that extends horizontally across processes that make up a value stream.

- Systems thinking is not an abstract exercise. Rather, it is essential in order to sustain superior performance. I believe there is now sufficient evidence for concluding that long-term firm performance is higher when employees are motivated to take responsibility to continuously improve the core processes, rather than when they are managed to meet accounting targets.

- The Toyota culture reflects a deep commitment, at all levels of the firm, to a knowing process based on Deming's Plan–Do–Check–Act learning cycle. The PDCA cycle is similar in many respects to the PAK Loop.

CHAPTER 7

Corporate Governance

*[T]he mindset of boards must move from one of careful review
to one of insatiable curiosity. . . . Question assumptions. . . .
Boards should take personal responsibility for understanding how
traditional budget processes and stretch goals frequently inculcate
a lack of integrity in an organization and destroy value. . . . Rarely
do board members have the kind of information they need to
assess accurately the progress of the corporation. Getting that
information requires boards to overhaul the process by which they
get substantive information about corporate performance from
one controlled by the CEO to one in which the board has ready
access to relevant information.*
—Michael C. Jensen and Joe Fuller, *Best Practices: Ideas and
Insights from the World's Foremost Business Thinkers*

In my view, a prerequisite for effective corporate governance is a systems
view of wealth creation that provides directors with needed clarity as
to how to execute their responsibilities. The main message in this chapter
is that a proposed Shareholder Value Review is a practical way to greatly
improve corporate governance and, in so doing, raise the public's trust in
free-market capitalism.

A SYSTEMS VIEW FOR CORPORATE GOVERNANCE

The board and management need a different knowledge base to guide their
top-level thinking. They need a more effective framework that connects

a firm's long-term financial performance to levels and changes in stock prices over time. Such a framework, or model, would offer a *common language* for communication among board members, management, employees, and shareholders that can more fruitfully address the complex managerial tasks involved in both achieving satisfactory near-term operating cash flows as well as securing long-term competitive advantage.

The board and management should not participate in Wall Street's extreme focus on the comparison of reported quarterly earnings against expected earnings. Decisions most likely to create long-term wealth (e.g., by promoting favorable fade rates), yet which may penalize short-term accounting results, should be made without hesitation, and the rationale for the decision explained to investors. When making resource allocation decisions, the firm must use an analysis focused on long-term wealth creation as the bedrock guide. This principle aligns the mutual, long-term interests of customers, employees, and shareholders.

Firms with a traditional, hierarchical command-and-control culture focused on short-term accounting results need to evolve toward a system that first and foremost focuses on human capital and on continual improvement to the business processes that generate a firm's long-term, financial performance. A widely shared culture of integrity, responsibility, and performance is essential for a firm to survive and prosper over the long term. A culture rooted in integrity and embraced by a diverse base of motivated employees should produce leaders within the firm who are both highly knowledgeable about the firm's businesses and capable of nurturing that culture in the future.

Consider a firm that has developed the "right" culture for nourishing teamwork, problem solving, and the mentoring of, and respect for, employees. In order to sustain that culture, the successor to today's CEO should be promoted from within the firm's pool of proven leaders. One would expect that a promoted-from-within CEO's compensation package would more likely be viewed as reasonable by employees and shareholders compared to a compensation package used to hire a star CEO from outside the firm.

CORPORATE GOVERNANCE NEEDS REPAIR

The perception of the performance of boards of directors certainly has suffered from the lack of effective board oversight during the late 1990s tech bubble and subsequent bear market. The bankruptcies of Enron, WorldCom, and the like heightened the widespread assumption that a key criterion for board membership is to be friends with the CEO.

The blowups of financial companies in 2008–2009 were further evidence that many boards do an inadequate job of monitoring management. Finally, both the public and shareholders in particular know in their gut that a corporate governance system awarding enormous paychecks to CEOs for average or below-average performance, and in some cases for being fired, is dysfunctional and rotten at the core.

Today's nomination and election process for directors is viewed as self-serving to management. The firm's owners (shareholders) should have a significant role in the composition of a board whose primary purpose is to oversee shareholders' interests. Boards with CEOs serving as the chair suggest that boards are acting to rubberstamp CEO decisions and are ill-positioned to fire an underperforming CEO. Does anyone expect a CEO/chairperson to open a board meeting by saying, "Let's have a frank talk about whether I am the best person to be leading this company"?

There is a growing movement to curtail management's influence over the board. Activities include attempts to prohibit CEOs from serving as board chair; allow shareholders to have more control over director nominations; require an annual up or down vote on specific directors; require nonbinding votes signaling approval or disapproval of top management's compensation; and prohibit poison-pill provisions that insulate management from market discipline via takeovers. In general, progress toward more implementation of shareholder rights has been slow.

The primary argument from many managements and boards for maintaining the status quo is that proposed changes would interfere with long-term wealth creation by giving too much power to investors whose valuation models use short-term time horizons. That seems to be a smoke screen because the plain fact is that CEOs want to either hand-pick board members, or at least have veto power over nominees. Since many board members are themselves CEOs, or former CEOs, the result is an all-too-common, implicit arrangement to not rock the boat, unless and until a firm's underperformance is so bad that it cannot be ignored. Nevertheless, it is a challenge to evolve toward a system of direct shareholder nomination of directors since, in theory, certain shareholders (e.g., union pension funds) might be motivated to seek directors whose primary mission is to benefit a favored constituency (union members).

How well does a CEO-dominated system work? For one bit of anecdotal evidence, consider the makeup of the ten external directors of Lehman

Brothers, a global Wall Street firm that went bankrupt as the 2008–2009 financial crisis unfolded. Of the ten directors, only two had experience in the financial services industry. Whatever knowledge these two directors had in the financial area was from an era before the latest innovations and global spread of complex derivatives and securitizations, with their attendant risks. What about the rest? Six retired CEOs, a retired Navy admiral, and a theater producer.

Walt Disney Company, under CEO Michael Eisner, had, at one time, three independent directors whose children were on the Disney payroll. As to the makeup of the board, Eisner said: "I would not suggest this board for a U.S. Steel, but if you are building theme parks, creating Broadway shows, and educating children, wouldn't you want a priest, a teacher, an architect, and an actor on your board?" (Craig, 2002). Experience in running a business to create long-term value, the ability to debate the CEO on resource allocation decisions, and knowledge about tying executive compensation to performance seems not to have been a strong suit of the board assembled by Eisner.

Perhaps what is needed is for more shareholders to follow the lead of television news anchor Howard Beale, the character played by Peter Finch in the 1976 movie *Network*. In reacting to the dismal condition of the economy, and society in general, he opened a window and screamed: "I'm mad as hell, and I'm not going to take this anymore!"

A very small minority of institutional shareholders seems motivated by such an attitude. Activist investors like Carl Icahn work hard to change how firms are managed and, in so doing, earn profits on their stock investments.

> Private enterprise forms the basis for our economy. It provides most of the jobs we enjoy and creates the wealth that raises living standards. New government spending can only do so much to repair the economy. Reshaping corporate management can do much more. . . . Faltering companies are now soaking up hundreds of billions of tax dollars, and they are not substantially changing their management structures as a price for taking this money.
>
> How does it serve the economy when we subsidize managements that got their companies into trouble? Where is the accountability? More importantly, where are the results? . . . *Nothing will do more to improve our economy than corporate governance changes.*
>
> (Icahn, 2009, italics added)

Shareholder activists invariably target firms that are widely acknowledged as being poorly managed and/or committed to a grow-the-business strategy that is unlikely to be economically rewarding. Often, boards in these situations have dug in their heels in support of top management. The shareholder activist is depicted as being interested only in short-term gains and not in building long-term shareholder value. The activist investor responds that by electing new directors, all shareholders would be better served. Missing from these corporate dramas is the big picture—how to get to an improved corporate governance system.

Carl Icahn is right in his assessment of the enormous potential benefit to economic growth that improved corporate governance would bring, and I have some thoughts about how to get there. I believe a three-step approach is needed that:

1. Makes very clear a standard of performance for boards
2. Involves a practical means for boards to demonstrate to shareholders that they are doing their job
3. Leads to a new era of corporate governance in which candidates for board membership are truly qualified and willing to commit the necessary time

A STANDARD OF PERFORMANCE FOR BOARDS

We think of a firm's CEO as being responsible for managing the firm so it survives and prospers over the long haul. But, the hiring, monitoring, and firing, if necessary, of CEOs is the responsibility of the board. Therefore, the ultimate responsibility for a firm's survival and prosperity rests with the board of directors.

The concepts presented in this book can be used to assemble a standard of performance for boards. In other words, investors can grade board performance on the three criteria described in the following. These same criteria can also serve as a scorecard for CEOs:

1. *A Culture of Integrity, Responsibility, and Performance that Is Focused on the Firm's Mission.* The firm's culture evolves as the aggregate of employees' experiences. The board and top management should promote ethical behavior (Frigo and Litman, 2008) within a work environment in which employees: do what they say they are going to do;

eagerly take responsibility to fix problems plus anticipate and remedy problems before they occur; view change as necessary to avoid obsolescence and to create new opportunities; and trust management to link compensation to one's contributions to improve overall system performance (Koch, 2007).

The firm's stated mission should inspire employees, as well as be "lived" at all levels throughout the firm. It should answer two questions: What kind of company do we want to create? How do employee commitments to the firm satisfy their need to gain knowledge and put that knowledge to good purpose? As a firm becomes increasingly diversified, a mission statement tends to have a less specific goal (vision) and instead stresses opportunities for commercial innovation and, in general, seeking optimum value from the firm's capabilities.

2. *Wealth-Creation Tasks.* Wealth creation is tied to management's strategic resource allocation decisions and to its skill in the execution of the five lean principles articulated in Chapter 6, namely, value specification for each product, value streams, flow, pull, and continuous pursuit of perfection. Success as a lean company requires a supportive culture and an information system attuned to the improvement of internal processes, not to financial reporting alone.

3. *Long-Term Financial Performance.* The reporting of financial performance should communicate the degree of success or failure with *past* wealth creation. Business strategies and major resource allocation decisions should be presented in terms of their expected contribution to *future* wealth creation. Interestingly, the more one becomes concerned with insights about wealth creation, the less useful are accounting earnings and the more useful is the life-cycle framework.

A SUCCESSFUL CULTURAL TRANSFORMATION EXAMPLE: EISAI CO., LTD.

Boards that monitor only financial performance are guaranteed to be late in recognizing serious systemic problems within the firm. Information flow to the board needs to include non-accounting variables that measure the efficiency of the processes that drive the financial results. The firm's culture is certainly an integral determinant of the employees' commitment to work more efficiently. A robust and widely shared culture of integrity, responsibility, and performance would seem to be a prerequisite to a firm achieving superior, long-term performance.

Recent work by Werner Erhard, Michael Jensen, and Steve Zaffron (2008) views *integrity* as important a factor of production as technology or knowledge. They see integrity as a potential source of outsized gains in organizational performance and, they say, "without integrity nothing works."

They define *integrity* to mean honoring your word, and *honoring your word* to mean "you either keep your word, or as soon as you know that you will not, you say you will not be keeping your word to those who were counting on your word and clean up any mess you caused by not keeping your word."

In their view, integrity is required in order to gain workability and the trust of others that in turn opens up the opportunity for high performance. In other words, the absence of integrity relegates the firm to no better than average long-term performance. Allan Scherr, who is also involved with this research, documented the importance of trust, based on his long-term managerial experience at IBM (Erhard, Jensen, and Zaffron, 2008, Appendix B).

Scherr noted that the loss of integrity within IBM was such that the group assigned to develop IBM's first personal computer felt that they could not depend on other groups within IBM to fulfill commitments they would make. Even though superior technologies needed for the PC existed in-house, the lack of trust resulted in IBM's personal computer group farming out development of the operating system to Microsoft and of the microchip to Intel. These enormous business opportunities were essentially gifted to Microsoft and Intel and forfeited by IBM because of IBM's defective culture.

A case study of the benefits from a radical improvement in Eisai Company, Ltd.'s culture is reported by Ikujiro Nonaka, Ryoko Toyama, and Toru Hirata in their excellent (2008) book, *Managing Flow: A Process Theory of the Knowledge-Based Firm*. During the 1990s, top management at Eisai Company, Ltd., a Japanese pharmaceutical company, undertook an enormous reorganization of the firm. The firm's culture was methodically changed to become aligned with a new mission—human health care, which the company refers to as *hhc*. Eisai employees now work to deliver benefits to patients and their families. That clear mission inspires attitudes and actions quite different from working with doctors and pharmacists in guiding the firm's direction.

To implement the mission, employees spend extensive time with patients and their families to deeply understand what is needed and why their work is important. Employees have enthusiastically embraced management's initiatives to work smarter and to share new knowledge widely within the firm.

Eisai management has created an environment in which the employees' success in doing their jobs translates into success in delivering the hhc mission. Employees feel that their job is to do good deeds, which is a powerful motivator. For example, by spending time with older patients, employees learned that the elderly have difficulty swallowing tablets because the body's production of saliva declines with age. This problem, and a host of other problems related to taking medicine, was solved with new products.

The transformation of Eisai took many years and produced a substantial improvement in CFROI returns, as shown in Figure 7.1.

Eisai is an example of the skillful execution of a long-term program to match the firm's mission to employee values; create and share knowledge; deliver significant innovations that directly benefit patients and, in so doing, reinforce the firm's culture; and ultimately, produce a track record of superior wealth creation.

Further, the history of Eisai is a reminder of the importance of the soft stuff—the culture and processes needed to deliver solid, long-term financial results. *Corporate governance needs to address the soft stuff as well as the hard financial numbers.* The next section outlines a new proposal for putting wealth-creation principles on center stage so that improved corporate governance can better evolve over time.

SHAREHOLDER VALUE REVIEW

The basic idea of a *Shareholder Value Review (SVR)* (Madden, 2007a, 2007b, 2008a) is for boards of directors to *demonstrate* that they are fulfilling their responsibility to shareholders—in short, to show that the board is a *facilitator of wealth creation.*

Broadly speaking, as noted earlier in this chapter, the board's performance in guiding and monitoring management can be gauged via the criteria of organizational structure and culture keyed to the firm's mission, wealth-creation tasks, and long-term financial results. What is needed is a practical tool to clearly communicate how boards are actually doing their job. That tool is an SVR.

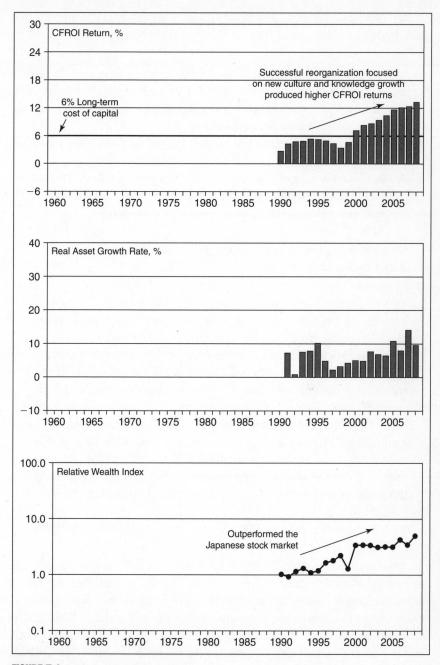

FIGURE 7.1   Eisai Company, Ltd.
Source: Credit Suisse HOLT ValueSearch® global database.

An SVR, consisting of the following three parts, needs to be included in annual reports:

1. A description of the *valuation model* that management and the board use to connect the firm's financial performance to its market value, plus a description of how the firm is organized and managed in order to nurture a performance-oriented culture
2. Consistent with this valuation model, graphs of *value-relevant track records* for the firm and each of its major business units
3. *Business unit analyses* that lay out how value has been created or reduced by each unit, along with the board's appraisal of management's strategy, and planned future investments for each unit

An SVR is similar in spirit to the board-directed strategic audit proposed by Gordon Donaldson:

> The mechanism is a formal strategic-review process . . . which imposes its own discipline on both the board and management, much as the financial audit process does. . . . An effective strategic-oversight process requires that the board take control not only of the criteria of performance but also of the database in which the criteria are maintained. One of the problems that outside board members often have in evaluating strategic performance is that all the information they receive passes through the filter of a management perspective. In addition, data often come with limited historical reference and in a format that does not map to the previous one. . . . The credibility of the board's review process depends on the integrity and consistency of the statistics by which progress is measured.
>
> (Donaldson, 1995)

As a practical matter, it will take pressure from pension fund trustees and institutional shareholders, at least initially, to convince the board and management to implement an SVR in the firm's annual report. That is because an SVR reflects a genuine transparency of managerial skill. Although management would be deeply involved in the development of track record displays, control of SVR data ultimately needs to be the board's responsibility for the reasons stated by Donaldson.

Valuation Model Selection

An SVR requires specificity about how the board and management connect financial performance to stock market valuation (i.e., a valuation model). By not carefully considering the criteria for an insightful and useful valuation model (see Chapter 5), the typical default model becomes a rule of thumb consisting of a price/earnings multiple and an earnings growth rate. Observations of a high correlation between quarterly earnings surprises and short-term moves in stock prices further cement the reliance on an earnings-centric valuation model.

Should not firms' chief financial officers (CFOs) be eager to educate management and the board as to the pitfalls of an excessive focus on short-term earnings as a wealth-creation compass? Apparently not; survey research shows that CFOs, for the most part, are committed to dancing to Wall Street's tune for quarterly earnings. Here is a sample of some survey results:

> Results . . . indicate that 80 percent of survey participants would decrease discretionary spending (e.g., R&D, advertising, maintenance) to meet an earnings target, even though many CFOs acknowledge that suboptimal maintenance and other spending can be value destroying. More than half of the CFOs (55.3 percent) said they would delay starting a new project to meet an earnings target, even if such a delay entailed a sacrifice in value. This evidence is interesting because CFOs appear to be willing to burn "real" cash flows for the sake of reporting desired accounting numbers.
>
> (Graham, Harvey, and Rajgopal, 2006, p. 31)

The missing ingredient here is an insightful valuation model that makes transparent the value-relevant components in firms' *track records* of financial performance. Absent these insights, attention gravitates toward a single earnings number. Consistent with this view, survey researchers noted: "*Lacking a sense of history*, analysts are prone to overreacting when the company misses an earnings target or when a new kink appears in the earnings path."

The proposed SVR does not dictate any particular valuation model or value-relevant track record format. One would expect firms to experiment with using earnings-centric valuation models. But keep in mind that an earnings-centric framework is conceptually flawed. Its deficiencies will become apparent when boards need to actually *explain* to investors, in detail, performance measurement and the long-term wealth creation or dissipation that has occurred.

A management fixated on earnings will make decisions with a careful eye on the likely impact on quarterly earnings. When the primary goal is increasing earnings, management can easily lose sight of the fundamental wealth-creation goal of achieving sustained economic returns in excess of the cost of capital. There are all sorts of ways to boost near-term earnings to the detriment of long-term wealth creation such as borrowing funds to invest in below-cost-of-capital projects that exceed the borrowing rate; or cutting back on research and development expenditures, maintenance outlays, and the like.

In addition, an extreme quarterly earnings orientation is ill-suited to nurture a culture of integrity and responsibility. *Motivating people to make targeted accounting numbers leads to gamesmanship and short-term expediencies—which is diametrically opposed to the five core lean principles rooted in a systems mindset for providing value to customers and reducing waste.*

In contrast to the problems with an earnings-centric approach, what benefits might be achieved from implementing some version of the life-cycle valuation model? In this regard, decades of experience with institutional money managers provided valuable lessons. After adopting the life-cycle model, an investment organization's portfolio managers and security analysts invariably improved in the following key areas:

- Clarity as to a firm's track record and the extent of past wealth creation or dissipation.
- Evaluation of management's resource allocation decisions (e.g., a below-cost-of-capital firm must, first and foremost, improve its economic returns).
- Quantification of the valuation impacts of alternative levels of future performance for a firm.
- Quantification of the long-term performance expectations implied in a firm's current stock price as well as its competitors' stock prices.
- Economic evaluation of mergers and acquisitions from the perspective of a firm's shareholders.
- Evaluation of how well top management's compensation is linked to wealth creation.

- Plausibility judgments of forecasts of a firm's future financial performance by comparison to the perceived skill level of firms that have historically delivered such performance.
- Approximation of a firm's economic returns from reported accounting data.

Many of these money management tasks are closely related to the tasks required of board members to fulfill their responsibility to shareholders. Keep in mind that money managers have their compensation and job security directly tied to the usefulness of the valuation models they choose to use. Consequently, life-cycle model adoption by these very discriminating users supports a prediction that corporations will also find this valuation model well suited to the needs of an SVR.

Finally, the first part of an SVR includes not only a description of the valuation model selected, but also a description of how the firm's organizational structure can nurture a viable, performance-oriented culture. These topics are related. That is, it is clearly advantageous to select a life-cycle model with track records that display long-term competitive fade rates. In this manner, investors can observe a relevant metric (fade rates) that is highly related to the firm's culture.

Value-Relevant Track Records

The second part of an SVR shows the value-relevant track records for the firm and its primary business units. If the firm chooses the life-cycle model, the complete package of variables needs to include:

- Economic asset base
- Economic returns compared to the cost of capital
- Reinvestment rates
- Fade (time series) patterns for economic returns and reinvestment rates

A board most likely would use consultants to guide their choice of a format and calculation routines for displaying the life-cycle variables. The displays serve as the launch pad for the board to handle the practical details of monitoring wealth creation. The data displays resolve Donaldson's concern that management-controlled data "often come with limited historical reference and in a format that does not map to the previous one."

A construction of track records begins with specifying economic assets for each business unit. Critically important intangibles that represent economic assets need to be added to a conventional accounting asset base. The capitalization of R&D expenditures is one example.

If SVRs gain widespread use, a lot of attention will be given to developing standards for handling intangibles. Eventually, this could lead to the handling of certain types of intangibles as part of conventional accounting principles. This would have the beneficial effect of standards evolving over time based on the practical experiences of those closest to the relevant data who are trying to make better wealth-creation decisions.

Economic returns and reinvestment rates for each business unit are a function of how economic assets are constructed. Although the life-cycle displays in Chapter 4 used a CFROI metric to estimate economic returns, this is not essential. Industrial firms, for example, may be more comfortable making economic adjustments to improve a conventional RONA (return-on-net-assets).

Estimating the next variable, cost of capital, poses a significant challenge. (Problems with mainstream finance's CAPM/Beta cost of capital were discussed in Chapter 5.) One choice is to begin with the long-term average of industrial or financial (as applicable) aggregate economic return as a proxy for the opportunity cost of capital. It is important to make the estimated cost of capital a visible line, plotted on the track record display, and to be aware of the impact of different cost-of-capital estimating procedures.

The critical guidepost to long-term wealth creation is the spread of economic returns as compared to the cost of capital. The spread—positive, zero, negative—determines whether, all else equal, reinvesting in the business will create additional wealth, have a neutral effect, or dissipate wealth. Reinvestment rates, measured as asset growth rates, get a boost from acquisitions. But, for most firms, the sustainability of future reinvestment rates depends on internally generated opportunities (i.e., *organic growth*), and consequently careful attention must be paid to the impact of acquisitions.[1] The preferred display of reinvestment rates would identify the contribution due to acquisitions (and divestitures).

One big advantage of life-cycle track records is the visual attention paid to competitive fade rates—the trends over time of economic returns and reinvestment rates. Long-term fade rates are the result of business processes (including knowledge creation and dissemination), culture, and strategies and speak volumes as to competitive advantage. As for purportedly gaining competitive advantage and boosting shareholder value, consultants often stress value-based management that involves a mindset of doing whatever it takes to improve short-term accounting targets. A helpful counterweight to such misguided short-termism is the long-term perspective of life-cycle track records and the need to grapple with the causes of long-term fade rates. This is exactly what was highlighted in the quotes of former Medtronic CEO, Bill George, in Chapter 4.

Business Unit Analyses

Value-relevant track records that position each business unit in a life-cycle context set the stage for the board to answer basic wealth-creation questions. For example, for startup business units: Is the amount of resources reinvested justified by progress in achieving nonfinancial milestones in relation to the size of the target market opportunity? For units earning well-above-cost-of-capital economic returns: What are the plans for expanding the business and fortifying that unit's competitive advantage? For mature businesses, stuck at a cost-of-capital plateau for economic returns: Is there a strategy in place to substantially improve economic returns that avoids the grow-the-business mindset that always gives top priority to a bigger market share regardless of the impact on wealth creation? If so, what is the strategy? For business units earning economic returns far below the cost of capital: Is downsizing planned, and, if not, why not? These questions deal with straightforward issues concerning financial results. Similar thinking is used by portfolio managers in assessing whether management really "gets" the fundamentals of shareholder value.

At a deeper level, the board should deal with the causes of long-term, financial results. The board's analyses of business units should communicate that they are engaged with an information system attuned to the improvement of internal processes. As said earlier, the processes that drive wealth creation are encapsulated in the five lean principles. If management's information system is simply made up of accounting control variables, there is a clear need for board involvement so the system can be improved.

The discussion of lean principles in Chapter 6 underscores how important it is to have a commitment at all levels of the firm to the wealth-creation process as well as a supportive corporate culture. The issue is well articulated by Jeffrey Pfeffer and Robert Sutton in their insightful book, *The Knowing–Doing Gap: How Smart Companies Turn Knowledge into Action*:

> [L]earning . . . is inhibited because companies are measuring the wrong things and not gathering data that permit them to really understand, manage, and control the process. In that regard, budgetary figures, costs, and even the balanced-scorecard measures are too far removed from processes in many instances to guide behavior and permit knowledge to be developed and turned into action.
>
> . . . But if there is one thing we know for certain, it is that organizations are systems in which behavior is interdependent. What you are able to accomplish, and indeed, what you choose to do and how you behave, is not solely under individual control. Rather, your behavior and performance are influenced by the actions, attitudes, and behaviors of many others in the immediate environment.
>
> . . . As long as accountants have control of internal measurements, not much will change. We have nothing against accountants, but are simply noting that they are pursuing a different set of goals. Specifically, we have seen few accountants or controllers who worry about the effect of measurement systems on turning knowledge into action or on the organization's ability to develop and transfer skill and competence.
>
> (Pfeffer and Sutton, 2000, p. 154–159)

Reply to SVR Objections

Board accountability to shareholders gives legitimacy to management's power. SVRs can orchestrate a new era of heightened transparency and accountability that would improve firms' long-term performance and investor trust. Nevertheless, CEOs who are intent on having the independence that comes with tight-fisted control of "their" boards will likely oppose SVRs, joined by those directors who are comfortable with the rituals of the status quo. The four principal objections most likely to be voiced by them are:

1. Directors lack sufficient in-depth knowledge of the firm's business units.
2. SVRs would force directors to deal with technical complexities of performance measurement for which they lack sufficient skill.
3. SVRs would be too costly to produce.
4. Competitors would benefit from SVR business unit disclosures.

As to knowledge of the firms' business units, management may be overly concerned with the trees and not appreciate the forest. That is, management typically is intent on producing results consistent with the existing strategy. In contrast, an SVR mindset encourages directors to raise broad, fundamental issues concerning different strategic opportunities that may deliver a more rewarding life-cycle performance for investors.

Capable directors have valuable experience that helps them focus on the big issues critical to failure or success. An SVR can lead both management and the board to a stronger conviction to take decisive actions as well as explain the rationale to investors. Directors who feel incapable of contributing to an SVR would seem to be unqualified to represent shareholder interests.

Regarding SVR technical complexities, the firm's auditors or a skilled consulting firm can provide the needed expertise. Whoever provides the technical support needs to report directly to the board, and not management. Of course, management would be intimately involved, which is a good thing, especially for the handling of accounting adjustments to estimate economic returns. *With an SVR, both management and the board would have a purpose in working with accounting data so as to better reflect economic reality and to avoid a blind reliance on conventional accounting principles as well as a tunnel focus on accounting earnings.*

The third criticism implies that any additional cost is bad. Yet, the actual relevant comparison is the total cost to shareholders versus the benefit to shareholders. Think of the cost to shareholders of the ineffective board oversight at Bethlehem Steel (see Figure 4.6). The potential gains from improved corporate governance are enormous. Further, over the long term, SVR-motivated participation by managements and boards in the development of new accounting principles to handle intangibles can promote even more wealth creation for the benefit of investors.

Another SVR benefit for investors is the likelihood of a lower cost of capital for the firm. The more uncertainty there is that a firm will grow the business with wealth-destroying reinvestments, or make expensive acquisitions that are not economically justified, then the higher the demanded return (cost of capital) by investors. SVR implementation is a step in the right direction to address this problem. In fact, those firms most in need of improved corporate governance should achieve the most favorable reduction in their cost of capital from SVR implementation.

This raises the valid point that especially well managed firms might only achieve a negligible gain from an SVR. To address this possibility, the board could allow shareholders an up or down vote on SVR implementation.

The fourth criticism is that upon observing wealth-creating economic returns for a business unit and reading a board's favorable assessment of that unit's prospects, competitors will pour additional resources into that area. This criticism implies that competitors are now largely clueless about success in the marketplace. My sense is that this perceived need for secrecy is unwarranted but it could delay or derail an SVR implementation.

One approach to counter it would be to implement an SVR using only data for the firm as a whole. While not my preferred choice, this still could lead to significant progress by instilling a viable wealth-creation framework at the board level. After some experience with a slimmed-down SVR, a board might later expand its SVR to include business unit analyses.

SVR as an Evolutionary Process

Over time, implementing an SVR would most likely lead to the following six benefits:

1. The life-cycle valuation model would gain widespread use as the deficiencies of the earnings-centric models became more visible.
2. Because they could more effectively explain their decisions to investors, managements and boards would be more willing to make long-term, wealth-creating investments that reduce near-term quarterly earnings.
3. A top-down board priority on having a robust information system would lead to more useful internal data and a greater concern for the five lean principles of wealth creation.
4. Extensible Business Reporting Language (XBRL) would be used to make available to investors the data used to produce life-cycle track records. The SEC has mandated that XBRL be used by firms to tag data according to highly specific definitions. This is the coming big thing to enable investors to perform customized security analyses. With XBRL, investors would understand how SVR track records were calculated (e.g., capitalization and amortization of R&D) and would be able to calculate track records using different assumptions, if they so desire.
5. In mismanaged companies, there would be earlier recognition by the board of a need to change course.
6. The nominating process for directors would increasingly emphasize individuals who are both motivated and skilled in performing the SVR tasks, which are fundamentally rooted in wealth creation (Acharya, Kehoe, and Reyner, 2009).

Summary of Key Ideas

■ Building anything, including long-term wealth, is better done when those involved speak a common language that facilitates the building process. Managements, boards, and investors would be well served by replacing an earnings-centric valuation language with the life-cycle language.

■ The core responsibility of the board of directors is to ensure that management nurtures a culture of integrity and responsibility and focuses on continual improvement of the processes that produce superior performance. This is necessary to avoid taking actions motivated by accounting targets and by a narrow grow-the-business mentality. Instead, wealth-creating strategies for each of the firm's business units should guide actions.

■ Shareholder Value Review is a practical means for board members to demonstrate that they are fulfilling their core responsibilities. Once the need for such a demonstration in the firm's annual report is recognized, the SVR's three components make eminent common sense: specification of a wealth-creation framework or model, display of value-relevant track records for the firm's business units, and explanation of how management's strategy and reinvestment for each business unit holds good potential for creating wealth.

■ SVRs represent a free-market approach to improving corporate governance. SVRs are voluntary even though, as a practical matter, pension fund trustees and institutional investors might initially need to nudge managements and boards to take action. In addition to addressing the core responsibilities of boards, SVRs would be a direct, hands-on purpose for managements and boards to better understand economic reality, to improve their decision making, and to share their experiences with accounting rule makers, thereby shaping the evolution of a new, more useful accounting system.

■ By bringing heightened transparency and accountability that would improve firms' long-term performance, SVRs would raise citizen trust in, and political support for, free-market capitalism.

CHAPTER 8

Concluding Thoughts

There is one fundamental insight underlying all management science. It is that the business enterprise is a system of the highest order: a system *whose parts are human beings contributing voluntarily of their knowledge, skill, and dedication to a joint venture. And one thing characterizes all genuine systems, whether they be mechanical like the control of a missile, biological like a tree, or social like the business enterprise: it is interdependence. . . . For what matters in any system is the performance of the whole; this is the result of growth and of dynamic balance, adjustment, and integration, rather than of mere technical efficiency.*

Primary emphasis on the efficiency of parts in management science is therefore bound to do damage. It is bound to optimize precision of the tool at the expense of the health and performance of the whole.

—Peter Drucker, *Management: Tasks, Responsibilities, Practices*
(emphasis in original)

Systems thinking entails an awareness of complexity and the pitfalls of a simplistic analysis of cause and effect. At times, a deeper appreciation for system complexity reveals the limitations of one's existing knowledge base and helps one to avoid changes that bring unintended, bad consequences. Other times, a systems mindset helps to put "stakes in the ground" delineating fundamental principles for dealing with a very complex system, such as a government regulatory environment or a large corporation.

Systems thinking can help public policy makers, business managers, and investors solve the very complex problems they face. The rest of this chapter highlights how application of systems thinking can benefit each of these groups of decision makers.

BENEFITS FOR PUBLIC POLICY MAKERS

Extensive, detailed, and rigid rules designed by politicians at some point in time invariably ignore a systems mindset and miss a design opportunity to incorporate feedback and learning over time. For example, financial reporting was put on center stage after the late 1990s tech bust and the bankruptcies of Enron and others. Due to public pressure to "fix the accounting fraud problem," Sarbanes-Oxley (SOX) legislation was passed. SOX represents a heavy-handed approach to changing behavior.

In mandating greatly expanded auditing requirements, SOX imposed significant additional financial costs that were especially burdensome for smaller firms. SOX required managements and boards to devote much more time to working with lawyers and accountants to ensure compliance with government rules (i.e., checking the boxes) (Perkins, 2007). This led to a heightened concern by managements for predictability and control. As such, a viable case can be made that an unintended consequence of SOX has been a dampening of growth in high-risk and high-innovation projects.

Since SOX became the law of the land, there has been a significant decline from the expected level of new public offerings from small, privately held firms. In no small measure is this due to the avoidance of the expensive SOX compliance costs that would result from becoming a public company.

SOX added complexity to an already enormously complex body of accounting rules. Moreover, SOX was essentially useless to both managers and investors in providing early warning signals of the coming blowup of financial companies in 2008. Ribstein and Butler (2008) argue for allowing shareholders to vote on whether their firm should incur the costs to comply with SOX. That is a very good idea.

We are better off with legislation and regulations based on a systems mindset geared to feedback and learning, with an awareness of the free-market efficiencies when people act to best meet their needs. Along these lines, recall the prior discussion of XBRL as a language to fundamentally restructure accounting by tagging highly detailed accounting data according to specific definitions. Users can then access a vast amount of data at a granular level and manipulate and analyze the data to suit their purposes.

Think for a moment about the potential benefits of the SEC-mandated implementation of XBRL. In contrast to 10-K reports displaying standardized aggregate data, sophisticated investors and data analysis firms serving less sophisticated investors would have the capability to drill down into a firm's accounting to assemble vastly more customized and accurate pictures of financial results. XBRL implementation would deal directly with the complexity problem and reduce the public perception of a need for additional bureaucratic controls while empowering individuals with information and a greater opportunity to learn.

Feedback from such an enhanced and transparent reporting system should favorably affect management behavior by: (1) minimizing opportunities to mislead outside investors by fulfilling the requirements of generally accepted accounting principles while simultaneously camouflaging the actual business economics (think Enron), and (2) recognizing more quickly increased risks that warrant immediate attention.

Would a fully developed and implemented XBRL regulatory environment have provided early recognition of the subprime mortgage debacle that the markets eventually recognized in late 2008? I believe it would have.

A centerpiece of the credit crisis was collateralized debt obligations (CDOs) that consisted of a pool of loans partitioned according to superficial assignments of risk by the rating agencies and sold as an investment. From the perspective of outside investors, individual loans in a CDO lost their identity. However, in an XBRL world, the relevant data about individual loans, including credit quality, would be tagged and not lost, even when those loans were repackaged into CDOs. From a systems perspective, an XBRL environment would enable investors to achieve faster and more effective PAK Loops in order to quickly unravel the complexities of CDOs and provide an order-of-magnitude more accurate perception of risk.

To sum up, regulations that promote feedback and fast learning have the genuine potential to minimize future crises like the credit debacle of 2008–2009. Such regulations would in turn minimize future heavy-handed government interventions in the private sector that invariably follow crises. In this regard, I believe the XBRL initiative being orchestrated by the Securities and Exchange Commission will produce benefits for the public greatly in excess of its costs.

BENEFITS FOR BUSINESS MANAGERS

After World War II, in order to survive, Toyota developed its lean management principles that form the core of its Toyota Production System. The lean principles discussed in Chapter 6 were not the result of some grand planning process. Rather, with a system goal of eliminating waste and providing value to customers, the Toyota Production System evolved over many decades. Toyota builds knowledge as much as it builds cars. Toyota plants operate in a manner that continually surfaces problems and expedites solutions. Its principal architect, Taiichi Ohno, had an extraordinarily intense and relentless focus on helping employees learn how to work more effectively.

As to standardized work in Toyota's plants, Ohno remarked:

> We start by adopting some kind—any kind—of work standards for a job. Then we tackle one improvement after another, trial and error. You could start by doing motion studies and time studies and whatever and try to come up with something perfect to start with, but that would never work. In the workplace, trying something immediately, even something imperfect, is always better than letting things sit while you refine a solution.
>
> (Shimokawa and Fujimoto, 2009, p. 9)

Of particular importance in the Toyota culture is dealing with problems by observing the situation first hand—that is, gaining a more accurate perception. In dealing with problems, Toyota employees are trained to "ask *why*" five times in order to more quickly discover the root cause of a problem that is hidden behind more obvious symptoms.

A necessary ingredient to superior long-term performance is a culture that promotes building knowledge. When a firm's employees consistently learn faster than its competitors, the likely result is long-term competitive advantage. Creating wealth is a long-term process because building knowledge is a long-term process. As noted earlier, building knowledge and creating wealth are opposite sides of the same coin.

Business educators and managements are increasingly looking at the practices of successful design firms for insights about *improving the knowing process in order to gain competitive advantage*. In addition to prototyping to achieve fast and effective PAK Loops, successful design firms place enormous importance on directly observing the customer experience—not unlike Toyota's focus on direct observations of problems in the workplace.

Roger Martin, Dean of the University of Toronto's Rotman School of Business, sees innovation as the big challenge for business and believes that the way forward is to fundamentally improve how business people think:

> When it comes to innovation, business has much to learn from design. The philosophy in design shops is, "try it, prototype it, and improve it." Designers learn by doing. The style of thinking in traditional firms is largely inductive—proving that something actually operates—and deductive—proving that something must be. Design shops add *abductive* reasoning to the fray—which involves *suggesting* that something *may be,* and reaching out to explore it. Designers may not be able to prove something *is* or *must be,* but they nevertheless reason that it *may be,* and this style of thinking is critical to the creative process. Whereas the dominant attitude in traditional firms is to see constraints as the enemy and budgets as the drivers of decisions, in design firms, the mindset is "nothing can't be done for sure" . . . . Business people don't need to understand designers better; *they need to be designers.*
>
> (Martin, 2004, p. 10, italics in original)

The key point is that the more one is concerned about creating wealth, the more attention is placed on the *process of building knowledge and putting that knowledge to use.* The unique ability of the ideal free market to coordinate knowledge building, resource allocation, and in fact the entire complex system of efficiently delivering value to consumers was described in Chapter 3. Recall that the free-market process has produced an extraordinary rise in the standard of living (see Figure 2.1), and this raises a question: How might a business firm duplicate this wealth-creation efficiency?

That question was answered by Charles Koch. In his aptly titled (2007) book, *The Science of Success: How Market-Based Management Built the World's Largest Private Company,* he describes a management philosophy that puts stakes in the ground for the very same principles that allow a free society to prosper. *Market-Based Management (MBM)* has been the way that Koch Industries has implemented a culture of integrity, responsibility, and performance.

MBM is a system that operates holistically and has five dimensions: vision, virtue and talents, knowledge processes, decision rights, and incentives. Charles Koch noted how this all evolved:

> I learned that prosperity is only possible in a system where property rights are clearly and properly defined and protected, people are free to speak, exchange and contract, and prices are free to guide beneficial action. Allowing people the freedom to pursue their own interests, within beneficial rules of just conduct, is the best and only sustainable way to promote societal progress.
>
> It seemed to me that these laws are fundamental not only to the well-being of societies, but also to the miniature societies of organizations. Indeed, that is what we found when we began to apply the laws systematically at Koch Industries.
>
> . . . MBM is not just another list of qualities of a successful company so common in today's management literature. It is a way for business to create a harmony of interest with society. For business to survive and prosper, it must create real long-term value in society through principled behavior.
>
> (Koch, 2007, p. ix–x)

The remarkable long-term success of Koch Industries suggests that both academics and corporate leaders should learn more about MBM (www.mbminstitute.org).

BENEFITS FOR INVESTORS

The stock market crash that began in late 2008 evaporated market valuations for many financial firms whose assets were, in hindsight, vastly overstated. Although one can expect better accounting disclosures from financial firms in the future and improved security analyses, many might well be wary of the ability of investors in the aggregate ("the market") to forecast company performance. Also, it is hard to deny that extreme optimism and pessimism gets baked into investor expectations for companies during the later stages of bubbles and crashes. Further, it is hard to deny that, in the short term, changes in firms' market valuations are highly correlated with quarterly earnings compared to what investors expected. So, it is no surprise that many managements and boards are skeptical of a finance theory that links firms' long-term financial performance to stock prices. Consequently, they rely heavily on an earnings-centric valuation model. But that results in corporate decisions that are highly influenced by their likely short-term effect, particularly on quarterly accounting earnings.

Given this environment, it may seem advisable that investors should be short-term oriented and spend a lot of their analytical effort on forecasting firms' upcoming quarterly earnings. I strongly disagree. Investors can profit by adopting the life-cycle valuation framework, using a long-term investment horizon, spending effort on judging managerial skill, and in particular, focusing on those situations where stock prices are moving in lockstep in response to short-term results—results that can differ markedly from the long-term performance that a firm seems capable of delivering. This recommendation is based on my own experience and, more importantly, the experiences of a large number of institutional portfolio managers and security analysts who use the life-cycle approach.

It is instructive to consider why many have adopted a short-term valuation model for stock prices. The heart of the matter takes us back to the beginning of this book and the components of the PAK Loop. *Feedback* about "how the market works" is largely comprised of short-term moves in individual stocks related to quarterly reports and the observed relationships between PE multiples and EPS growth rates for firms. This leads to a *knowledge base* comprised of assumptions about quarterly earnings surprises and stock price changes, plus earnings growth rates and PE multiples—the short-term, earnings-centric valuation model. In that world view, *perceptions* about how the world works are driven by observations of short-term changes in stock prices.

While concerned about short-term changes, many institutional portfolio managers and security analysts have an added *purpose* that impacts their perceptions and feedback. They are concerned with the levels of stock prices—that is, the correspondence between a firm's actual market valuation and a warranted valuation based on a long-term forecast of a firm's anticipated net cash receipts. This has led to the widespread adoption of the life-cycle valuation model in the money management industry.

Chapter 5 reviewed how warranted value calculations are generated by forecasts of the four life-cycle variables: economic returns, cost of capital, reinvestment rates, and fade rates. Extensive experience by money management professionals with the life-cycle variables in analyzing a large universe of companies on a worldwide basis has demonstrated its superiority over the short-term earnings-centric valuation model. Some sense of the usefulness of the life-cycle approach for understanding both levels and changes in stock prices over the long term is gained by studying the company examples presented in Chapters 4, 5, and 6. With the life-cycle framework, a useful way to interpret quarterly results is within the context of a firm's life-cycle track record and plausible scenarios as to future life-cycle performance.

The life-cycle framework works especially well in assisting analysts, portfolio managers, and investors to identify key valuation issues and the related managerial tasks to enhance shareholder value. Experience in using this framework leads to improved plausibility judgments about one's own forecasts, the forecasts of others, and the forecasts embedded in today's stock prices for companies. Judging the degree of difficulty in achieving forecasted levels of performance is greatly aided by a comparison to the type of companies that have achieved such levels of life-cycle performance. Along with its value as an analytical tool, the life-cycle framework provides a more effective language for communicating wealth creation issues.

There are three interrelated conceptual pillars to understanding wealth creation: (1) a systems mindset, (2) the knowledge building process (PAK Loop), and (3) the firms' competitive life cycle. They lead to deeper understanding of cause and effect that helps investors think more productively. In particular, with a systems mindset and the knowledge building process one can more easily pinpoint especially crucial assumptions that are part of a firm's business strategy or embedded in its culture. These assumptions could foster innovation, with potential for big rewards, or could constrain performance and impede needed change.

At one level of thinking, a firm's stock price history will make a great deal more economic sense when the firm's accounting results are expressed as a life-cycle track record. At a deeper level, one wants to know why, for example, a particular firm has delivered dramatically better or worse long-term competitive fade compared to its industry peers. Consider the strategic decision by the management of Southwest AirLines to reject the widely accepted industry assumption that efficient operation of planes required a hub and spoke airport structure. Management paid attention to a total system focused on value to the customer who wants to get from A to B without the hassle of going through a hub. With the increased demand from customers for its low fares and direct flights and with its customer-centric culture and high operational efficiency, Southwest Airlines' profits typically exceed the total profits of all its U.S. competitors. The sharper an analyst, portfolio manager, or investor becomes in understanding the past, the better equipped they are to analyze today's investment opportunities.

Finally, as to my proposal for improving corporate governance through implementation of the Shareholder Value Review, I have two predictions. First, boards of directors and top managements that commit to SVR using a life-cycle framework will be pleasantly surprised by the positive response from institutional shareholders and by a more useful dialogue with the investment community.

Second, SVR will facilitate firms' making long-term investments that penalize quarterly results in direct proportion to the level of managerial skill demonstrated in firms' track records. Managements that have clearly proven their ability to earn economic returns well in excess of the cost of capital give investors a strong reason to be patient for future rewards and accept any near-term shortfalls in quarterly earnings. In some cases, I would not be surprised if these types of companies see a rise in their stock prices upon announcement that their upcoming quarter will be less than expected due to a very large investment outlay. However, those managements that have steadfastly failed to earn the cost of capital and then announce a major capital outlay that will hurt near-term earnings should not expect a favorable reaction from investors.

By focusing on the firm's level of managerial skill as demonstrated in long-term track records, the Shareholder Value Review offers an evolutionary path for achieving genuine accountability and transparency regarding corporate performance and for making progress in restoring the public's trust in, and support for, free-market capitalism. There is no more important place for sound thinking on wealth-creation principles than the boardrooms of corporate America.

Notes

CHAPTER 1   A Systems Mindset

1. I have found it uniquely valuable to experience many of the Ames demonstrations. For me, the direct experience was exceedingly more useful than having read about the demonstrations. Consider participating in these demonstrations by visiting the Exploratorium, a museum of science, art, and human perception, in San Francisco.

2. For one practical proposal for how society could benefit from quicker trips through the PAK Loop, see "A Dual Track System to Give More-Rapid Access to New Drugs: Applying a Systems Mindset to the US Food and Drug Administration (FDA)," (Madden 2009b). Also see Madden (2005b).

3. In his book, *Behavior: The Control of Perception*, William Powers postulates that human beings, indeed all organisms, function as control systems with three basic functions: action, perception, and comparison. Importantly and uniquely, Powers describes a structure by which neural cells and circuits could so function. While much has been learned about where in the brain certain functions seem to occur, the overall process is often said to be a "mystery."

   We do not plan, in the usual sense, the actions necessary for control; rather, we act to control the consequences, which we individually experience as perceptions. When in a specific context an individual compares his actual, or input, perception with his desired, or reference, perception and detects a mismatch (or error), action is taken to attempt to bring the actual perception into alignment with the reference perception. Hence, behavior: the control of perception.

   PCT (Perceptual Control Theory) is based on a hierarchy of control systems. Higher-level systems set reference points (what to perceive) for lower-level (faster-reacting) systems. Mismatches of input perception and reference perceptions are handled at the lowest level of perception and control sufficient for the situation. The lowest-level systems deal with intensity and sensation, whereas the highest levels deal with principles of behavior and core values. Powers notes that a control system hierarchy reflects the best features of reflex action and cognitive planning:

   The higher systems, rather than telling the lower ones *how to act*, tell the lower systems *what to perceive*. It is up to the lower systems to produce whatever actions are required to make the real perception match the reference perception. This means that the higher systems don't have to plan what to do in case of disturbances; if the lower systems can take care of the disturbances, they will do so without being told. On the other hand, the higher systems can *change* the reference conditions for the lower systems, so unlike a reflex system, the lower systems can show different behaviors under the same circumstances.

(Powers, 1998, pp. 40–41, italics in original)

PCT offers clear and compelling explanations for all sorts of human activities (see www.perceptualcontroltheory.org). For example, PCT explanations of how one walks or drives a car are eminently more plausible than alternatives that involve planning actions in advance. Particularly important is the growing body of experimental demonstrations (Powers, 2008) leaving little ambiguity that tested behavior conforms to PCT (see www.mindreadings.com). And the experiments do not depend on statistical sampling, which is inappropriate when the objective is to learn about how *every* human behaves. PCT appears to reflect a basic way in which human beings function.

PCT has had limited impact thus far on conventional thought in psychology and other fields dealing with human behavior in individuals or in groups. One reason is that it would require a complete overhaul of social science research methods because its application would require explicit testing to identify control variables of the human subjects (Marken, 2009). To identify control variables, a researcher must apply different disturbances to aspects of the environment that possibly are being controlled (reference perceptions) and then look for a lack of an effect from these disturbances, which would indicate that individuals are varying their behavior in order to maintain a desired reference perception. The difficulty of identifying control variables increases exponentially as situations become more complex.

CHAPTER 3   The Ideal Free-Market System

1. The description of a free-market system is adapted from Madden (2005a), Chapter 2, "Economic Progress."

CHAPTER 4   The Competitive Life-Cycle View of the Firm

1. Parts of this chapter are adapted from Madden (2005a, 2007b, and 2009a).
2. For the period 1960 to 1996, aggregate U.S. industrial CFROI returns approximated 6 percent real, and a "market-derived" real discount rate (see Chapter 5), or cost of capital, also averaged approximately 6 percent real (Madden, 1999, p. 92). For the nonfinancial sector, 1950 to 1996, Fama and French (1999) estimated the real cost of capital at 5.95 percent and the return on corporate assets, unadjusted for inflation, at 7.38 percent.
3. In almost every year since 1985, the firm has recorded substantial restructuring charges (included in CFROI return calculations). Since 1990, as shown in the middle panel of Figure 4.2, big negative asset growth rates reflect divestitures of assets as the firm belatedly changed its strategy.

4. The mechanisms by which Big Steel attempted to insulate itself from competition from 1969 to 1992 included: voluntary restraint agreements (VRAs) from 1969 to 1974, a Trigger Price Mechanism from 1978 to 1982, and a decade of new VRAs from 1982 to 1992. Barringer and Pierce (2000) estimate that the total cost to American consumers from higher prices from 1969 to 1992 was in the range of $90 to $151 billion dollars, expressed in 1999 dollars. This converts to $113 to $190 billion in 2008 dollars. There were 67.2 million American family households in 1992. Consequently, the range translates to about $1,700 to $2,800 per American family, expressed in 2008 dollars.

CHAPTER 5   The Life-Cycle Valuation Model as a Total System

1. Parts of this chapter are adapted from Madden (2009a).
2. Acquisition goodwill and R&D capitalization were two important research areas that were still in progress when my 1999 book was published. The 1999 CFROI return calculation included goodwill and ignored R&D capitalization. Subsequent work showed the importance of measuring CFROI returns without goodwill in order to gauge likely future returns from investments in operating assets. This became the basic CFROI metric. Yet the former method for calculating a CFROI return was retained as an alternative measure in order to hold management accountable for the full price paid for acquisitions. Where applicable, both are now shown in track record displays. Also, routines were developed to estimate a life for R&D in different industries, and this enabled capitalized R&D to be included in the asset base of companies having substantial R&D outlays.
3. With a more accurate valuation of the wind-down of existing assets used in a valuation model, users then need to forecast ROIs on future, *incremental* investments each year. An argument to use less fine-grained computations for existing assets is certainly defensible if the user has limited information. This would often be the case for outside investors compared to a firm's management. One instance, though, where sophisticated outside investors perform extensive analysis on existing assets is distressed companies that are candidates for bankruptcy.
4. With a 15-year project life, it takes 15 years to build up a full portfolio of projects that then generate the financial statements used to calculate the plotted Earnings/Common Equity and the CFROI returns.
5. Investors who use the life-cycle valuation model are familiar with the algorithms used to forecast long-term NCRs. For investment decisions on companies, they rely heavily on comparing standard fade forecasts versus current market-implied expectations for fade. At times, investors input their own judgments about fade that tend to be minor variations of the standard fade forecasts. As a practical matter, the NCR forecasts used by investors are consistent with the NCR forecasts used to obtain company-specific, market-derived discount rates.

6. Starting in 2008, Taiwanese companies are required to expense stock bonuses.

7. To reduce the volatility due solely to year-to-year changes in deferred taxes, the CFROI return uses as-reported income taxes and not cash taxes. This enabled better fade forecasts to be made from the use of past CFROI variability. Nevertheless, a pure measure of an economic return would use cash taxes paid.

8. More recent research at Credit Suisse HOLT has provided empirical evidence that a near-term fade window longer than five years is appropriate for companies with certain characteristics.

9. My empirical study of CFROI fade (summarized in Madden, 1999, pp. 165–167) used a sample of 1,000 industrial companies that were ranked high-to-low on CFROI return at the beginning and end of four-year time periods. Fade was measured as the change in rank. Although this is an admittedly coarse instrument to use, these original findings were later replicated with econometric studies at Credit Suisse HOLT on long-term time periods for both U.S. and non-U.S. companies.

10. Friedman's (1953) methodology of positive economics promoted the view that the realism of assumptions is immaterial as long as the world behaves as if the assumptions were true. This gave added credibility to mathematical models such as the CAPM, and deflected criticism of the use of empirically untested assumptions (Frankfurter and McGoun, 1996).

    In the final section of an article about research methodology (Madden, 1991), I argued that Friedman's methodology of positive economics interfered with the process of feedback-theory improvement. I sent the article to Friedman and in a letter (Friedman, 1990) he replied: "I have read your final section, I have no quarrel with it, and it has no quarrel with me. . . ." I conclude that, on one hand, Friedman appreciates how mathematical theorizing in economics, greatly facilitated by the use of unrealistic assumptions, has arguably been excessive (Coase, 1995). On the other hand, Friedman believes that his own application of the methodology of positive economics has simplified highly complex phenomena in a useful way.

11. For insights on new approaches to researching levels and changes in stock prices over time, see the work of Rawley Thomas contained in various chapters in *The Valuation Handbook* (Gup and Thomas, 2009).

12. Research by Hewitt Associates (Ubelhart, 2007) has linked human capital investments to subsequent changes in financial performance (measured as changes in CFROI returns) based on a proprietary database of 20 million employees in 1,000 large companies. A metric was developed that measures the effectiveness of a firm's human resource policies in the attraction and retention of pivotal (higher-pay-grade) employees, and it appears to have predictive value for future financial performance. This research is important because it shows that investments in human capital can be quantified in terms of a financial return on investment. See www.evidence-basedmanagement.com/guests/ubelhart_jan07.html.

CHAPTER 7 Corporate Governance

1. For the purpose of using past levels and trends in economic returns to help gauge likely economic returns on future investments, it is helpful for economic returns to be calculated based on operating assets stripped of acquisition goodwill. Alternatively, management should be held accountable for the full purchase prices of acquisitions and that requires the inclusion of acquisition goodwill. Consequently, imposition of a single treatment for acquisition goodwill will cause problems (Eddins and Madden, 2002).

References

Acharya, Viral V., Conor Kehoe, and Michael Reyner. 2009, March. "Private Equity vs. PLC Boards in the UK: A Comparison of Practices and Effectiveness." ECGI-Finance working paper no. 233/2009, http://ssrn.com/abstract=1324019.

Aghion, Philippe, Yann Algan, Pierre Cahuc, and Andre Shleifer. 2009, January. "Regulation and Distrust." NBER working paper no. 14648.

Alessandri, Todd M., David N. Ford, Diane M. Lander, Karyl B. Leggio, and Marilyn Taylor. 2004. "Managing Risk and Uncertainty in Complex Capital Projects." *Quarterly Review of Economics and Finance* 44(5, December): 751–767.

Argyris, Chris, and Donald A. Schön. 1996. *Organizational Learning II: Theory, Method, and Practice.* Boston: Addison-Wesley.

Bacon, John U. 2004. *America's Corner Store: Walgreens' Prescription for Success.* Hoboken, NJ: John Wiley & Sons, 2004.

Baetjer, Howard, and Peter Lewin. 2007, April. "Can Ideas Be Capital?: Can Capital Be Anything Else?" Mercatus Center, George Mason University.

Bamberger, W. C. 2006. *Adelbert Ames, Jr.: A Life of Vision and Becomingness.* Whitmore Lake, MI: Bamberger Books.

Barringer, William H., and Kenneth J. Pierce. 2000. *Paying the Price for Big Steel.* American Institute for International Steel.

Baumol, William J. 2002. *The Free-Market Innovation Machine: Analyzing the Growth Miracle of Capitalism.* Princeton, NJ: Princeton University Press.

Baumol, William J. 2008. "Entrepreneurship: Productive, Unproductive, and Destructive." In Benjamin Powell, ed., *Making Poor Nations Rich: Entrepreneurship and the Process of Economic Development.* Stanford, CA: Stanford University Press.

Bebchuk, Lucian, and Jesse Fried. 2004. *Pay without Performance: The Unfilled Promise of Executive Compensation.* Cambridge, MA: Harvard University Press.

Beinhocker, Eric D. 2006. *The Origin of Wealth: Evolution, Complexity, and the Radical Remaking of Economics.* Boston: Harvard Business School Press.

Bhidé, Amar. 2008. *The Venturesome Economy: How Innovation Sustains Prosperity in a More Connected World.* Princeton, NJ: Princeton University Press.

Black, William. 2009. "The Lessons of the Savings-and-Loan Crisis." Interview, *Barron's* 13 (April): 36–37.

Bogle, John. 2009. "Markets in Crisis." Interview, *Financial Analysts Journal* 65 (1, January/February): 17–24.

Bookstaber, Richard. 2007. *A Demon of Our Own Design.* Hoboken, NJ: John Wiley & Sons.

Brealey, Richard A., Stewart C. Myers, and Franklin Allen. 2006. *Principles of Corporate Finance,* 8th ed. New York: McGraw-Hill Irwin.

Brown, Tim. 2007. "Strategy by Design," *Fast Company* (December 19, 2007).

CAIB (*Columbia* Accident Investigation Board) Report. 2003. Six volumes: Vol. 1. Washington, DC: Government Printing Office. At www.caib.us/news/report/default.html.

Cantril, Hadley. 1950. *The "Why" of Man's Experience*. New York: Macmillan Company, p. 59.

Cantril, Hadley. 1960. *The Morning Notes of Adelbert Ames, Jr*. New Brunswick, NJ: Rutgers University Press.

CFA Institute. 2005. *A Comprehensive Business Reporting Model: Financial Reporting for Investors*.

Christensen, Clayton M. 1997. *The Innovator's Dilemma: When New Technologies Cause Great Firms to Fail*. Boston: Harvard Business School Press.

Coase, R. H. 1995. *Essays on Economics and Economists*. Chicago: University of Chicago Press.

Collins, Jim. 2001. *Good to Great: Why Some Companies Make the Leap . . . and Others Don't*. New York: HarperBusiness.

Copeland, Tom, and Aaron Dolgoff. 2005. *Outperform with Expectations-Based Management: A State-of-the-Art Approach to Creating and Enhancing Shareholder Value*. Hoboken, NJ: John Wiley & Sons.

Corcam, Robert. 2002. *Boyd: The Fighter Pilot Who Changed the Art of War*. New York: Litle, Brown and Company.

Corrado, Carol, John Haltiwanger, and Daniel Sichel. 2005. *Measuring Capital in the New Economy*. Chicago: University of Chicago Press.

Craig, Michael. 2002. "Magic Kingdom Come." At http://spectator.org/archives/2002/08/15/magic-kingdom-come.

DeLong, J. Bradford. 2000. "Cornucopia: The Pace of Economic Growth in the Twentieth Century." NBER working paper no. 7602. At www.j-bradford-delong.net/TCEH/2000/TCEH_2.html.

DeLuzio, Mark. 2001. "Danaher Is a Paragon of Lean Success." Interview, *Manufacturing News* 8(12, June 29, 2001).

Dettmer, H. William. 2007. *The Logical Thinking Process: A Systems Approach to Complex Problem Solving*. Milwaukee, WI: ASQ Quality Press.

Donaldson, Gordon. 1995. "A New Tool for Boards: The Strategic Audit." *Harvard Business Review* (July/August): 99–107.

Drucker, Peter F. 1993. *Management: Tasks, Responsibilities, Practices*. New York: Collins Business, p. 508.

Eddins, Sam. 2009, March. "Tax Arbitrage Feedback Theory." Working paper. At http://ssrn.com/abstract=1356159.

Eddins, Sam, and Bartley J. Madden. 2002. "Will Your Next Acquisition Pay Off?" *Shareholder Value* (May/June).

Erhard, Werner H., Michael C. Jensen, and Steve Zaffron. 2008, April. "Integrity: A Positive Model that Incorporates the Normative Phenomena of Morality, Ethics, and Legality." Working paper. At http://ssrn.com/abstract=920625.

Fabozzi, Frank J., Sergio M. Focardi, and Caroline Jones. 2008. *Challenges in Quantitative Equity Management*. Charlottesville: Research Foundation of CFA Institute.

Fama, E. F., and K.R. French. 1999. "The Corporate Cost of Capital and the Return on Corporate Investment." *Journal of Finance* 54(6, December): 1939–1967.

Fama, E. F., and K. R. French. 2000. "Forecasting Profitability and Earnings." *Journal of Business* 73(2, April): 161–175.

Fama, E. F., and K. R. French. 2004. "The Capital Asset Pricing Model: Theory and Evidence." *Journal of Economic Perspectives* 18(3, Summer): 25–46.

Fiume, Orest. 2007. "Lean Strategy and Accounting: The Roles of the CEO and CFO." In Joe Stenzel, ed., *Lean Accounting: Best Practices for Sustainable Integration*. Hoboken, NJ: John Wiley & Sons, pp. 43, 46–47.

Forrester, Jay W. 1969. *Urban Dynamics*. Cambridge, MA: MIT Press, p. 107.

Frankfurter, George M., and Elton G. McGoun. 1996. *Toward Finance with Meaning—The Methodology of Finance: What It Is and What It Can Be*. Greenwich, CT: JAI Press.

Friedman, Milton. 1962. *Capitalism and Freedom*. Chicago: University of Chicago Press, p. 15.

Friedman, Milton. 1990. Personal correspondence (April 3, 1990).

Frigo, Mark L., and Joel Litman. 2008. *Driven: Business Strategy, Human Actions, and the Creation of Wealth*. Chicago: Strategy & Execution, LLC.

Gazzaniga, Michael S., Richard B. Ivry, and George R. Mangun. 2008. *Cognitive Neuroscience: The Biology of the Mind*, 3rd ed. New York: W.W. Norton.

George, Bill. 2003. *Authentic Leadership: Rediscovering the Secrets to Creating Lasting Value*. San Francisco: Jossey-Bass.

George, Bill. 2007. *True North: Discover Your Authentic Leadership*. Hoboken, NJ: John Wiley & Sons.

Gerstner, Louis V. 2002. *Who Says Elephants Can't Dance?: Inside IBM's Historic Turnaround*. New York: HarperBusiness.

Gilbert, Clark G., and Clayton Christensen. 2005. "Anomaly-Seeking Research: Thirty Years of Development in Resource Allocation Theory." In Joseph L. Bower and Clark G. Gilbert, eds., *From Resource Allocation to Strategy*. Oxford: Oxford University Press.

Goldratt, Eliyahu M., and Jeff Cox. 2004. *The Goal: A Process of Ongoing Improvement*, 3rd ed. Great Barrington, MA: North River Press.

Graham, John R., Campbell R. Harvey, and Shivaram Rajgopal. 2006. "Value Destruction and Financial Reporting Decisions." *Financial Analysts Journal* 62(6, November/December): 27–39.

Gup, Benton, and Rawley Thomas, eds. 2009. *The Valuation Handbook*. Hoboken, NJ: John Wiley & Sons.

Gwartney, James, and Robert Lawson. 2008. *Economic Freedom of the World: 2008 Annual Report*. Fraser Institute.

Hamm, Steve, and William C. Symonds. 2006. "Mistakes Made on the Road to Innovation." *Business Week* 27(November).

Hammond, Grant T. 2001. *The Mind of War: John Boyd and American Security*. Washington: Smithsonian Books.

Hand, J., and B. Lev, eds. 2003. *Intangible Assets: Values, Measures, and Risks*. Oxford: Oxford University Press.

Haugen, Robert A. 1999. *The New Finance: The Case Against Efficient Markets*, 2nd ed. Upper Saddle River, NJ: Prentice Hall, pp. 139–140.

Hayek, F. A. 1945. "The Use of Knowledge in Society." *American Economic Review* 35(4, September): 519–530.

Healy, Paul M., Stewart C. Myers, and Christopher D. Howe. 2002. "R&D Accounting and the Tradeoff between Relevance and Objectivity." *Journal of Accounting Research* 40(3, June): 677–710.

Heuer, Richards J. 1999. *Psychology of Intelligence Analysis*. Government Printing Office. Free download at www.cia.gov/library/center-for-the-study-of-intelligence/csi-publications/books-and-monographs/psychology-of-intelligence-analysis/psychofintelnew.pdf.

Holmes, Kim R., Edwin J. Feulner, and Mary Anastia O'Grady. 2008. *2008 Index of Economic Freedom*. Heritage Foundation and Dow Jones & Company.

Hopp, Wallace J., and Mark L. Spearman. 2004. "To Pull or Not to Pull: What Is the Question?" *Manufacturing & Service Operations Management* 6(2, Spring): 133–148.

Huntzinger, Jim. 2007. "Limited Production Principles: Right-Sizing for Effective Lean Operations and Cost Management." In Joe Stenzel, ed., *Lean Accounting: Best Practices for Sustainable Integration*. Hoboken, NJ: John Wiley & Sons.

Icahn, Carl C. 2009. "The Economy Needs Corporate Governance Reform." *Wall Street Journal* (January 23, 2009).

Ittelson, William H., and Franklin P. Kilpatrick. 1951. "Experiments in Perception." *Scientific American* (August): 50–55.

Iverson, Ken. 1998. *Plain Talk: Lessons from a Business Maverick*. Hoboken, NJ: John Wiley & Sons.

Jensen, Michael C., and Joe Fuller. 2003. "What's a Director to Do?" In *Best Practices: Ideas and Insights from the World's Foremost Business Thinkers*. Cambridge, MA: Perseus Publishing.

Johnson, H. Thomas. 2007. "Lean Dilemma: Choose System Principles or Management Accounting Controls—Not Both." In Joe Stenzel, ed., *Lean Accounting: Best Practices for Sustainable Integration*. Hoboken, NJ: John Wiley & Sons.

Johnson, H. Thomas, and Anders Bröms. 2000. *Profit beyond Measure: Extraordinary Results through Attention to Work and People*. New York: Free Press.

Johnson, Mark W., Clayton M. Christensen, and Henning Kagermann. 2008. "Reinventing Your Business Model." *Harvard Business Review* (December): 51–59.

Kaufman, Stuart A. 2008. *Reinventing the Sacred: A New View of Science, Reason and Religion*. New York: Basic Books.

Koch, Charles G. 2007. *The Science of Success: How Market-Based Management Built the World's Largest Private Company*. Hoboken, NJ: John Wiley & Sons.

Larsen, Tom, and David Holland. 2008. "Beyond Earnings: A User's Guide to Excess Return Models and the HOLT CFROI® Framework." In Jan Viebig, Thorsten Poddig, and Armin Varmaz, eds., *Equity Valuation: Models from Leading Investment Banks*. Hoboken, NJ: John Wiley & Sons.

Leeson, Peter T. 2009, July. "Two Cheers for Capitalism?" Working paper, Economics Department, George Mason University.

Leonard, Dorothy, and Walter Swap. 2004. "Deep Smarts." *Harvard Business Review* (September): 88–97.

Lewis, William W. 2004. *The Power of Productivity: Wealth, Poverty, and the Threat to Global Stability*. Chicago: University of Chicago Press.

Linzmayer, Owen W. 2004. *Apple Confidential 2.0: The Definitive History of the World's Most Colorful Company*. San Francisco: No Starch Press.

Loomis, Carol J. 2004. "The Sinking of Bethlehem Steel." *Fortune* (April 5, 2004).

Madden, Bartley J. 1991. "A Transactional Approach to Economic Research." *Journal of Socio-Economics* 20(1): 57–71.

Madden, Bartley J. 1996. "The CFROI Life Cycle." *Journal of Investing* (Summer).

Madden, Bartley J. 1998. "The CFROI Valuation Model." *Journal of Investing* (Spring).

Madden, Bartley J. 1999. *CFROI Valuation: A Total System Approach to Valuing the Firm*. Butterworth-Heinemann.

Madden, Bartley J. 2005a. *Maximizing Shareholder Value and the Greater Good*. Naperville: LearningWhatWorks, Inc.

Madden, Bartley J. 2005b. "A Clinical Trial for the Food and Drug Administration's Clinical Trial Process." *Cancer, Biotherapy & Radiopharmaceuticals* 20(6): 569–578.

Madden, Bartley J. 2007a. "For Better Corporate Governance, the Shareholder Value Review." *Journal of Applied Corporate Finance* 19(1, Winter): 102–114.

Madden, Bartley J. 2007b. "Guidepost to Wealth Creation: Value-Relevant Track Records." *Journal of Applied Finance* (Fall/Winter): 119–130.

Madden, Bartley J. 2008a. "Shareholder Value Reviews." *Strategic Finance* (September).

Madden, Bartley J. 2008b. "Systems Mindset." Powerpoint presentation, LearningWhatWorks, Inc.

Madden, Bartley J. 2009a. "Applying a Systems Mindset to Stock Valuation." In Benton Gup and Rawley Thomas, eds., *The Valuation Handbook: Valuation Techniques of Today's Top Practitioners*. Hoboken, NJ: John Wiley & Sons.

Madden, Bartley J. 2009b. "A Dual Track System to Give More-Rapid Access to New Drugs: Applying a Systems Mindset to the U.S. Food and Drug Administration (FDA)." *Medical Hypotheses* 72: 116–120.

Marken, Richard S. 2009. "You Say You Had a Revolution: Methodological Foundations of Closed-Loop Psychology." *Review of General Psychology*, 13(2): 137-145.

Martin, Roger. 2004. "The Design of Business." *Rotman Management* (Winter): 7–10.

Mill, John S. 2004. *Principles of Political Economy*. Amherst: Promethus Books.

Miller, Paul B. W., and Paul R. Bahnson. 2007. "The Top 10 Reasons to Fix the FASB's Conceptual Framework." *Strategic Finance* (July): 43–49.

Mokyr, Joel. 2002. *The Gifts of Athena: Historical Origins of the Knowledge Economy*. Princeton, NJ: Princeton University Press.

Moore, Stephen. 2008. "Washington Is the Problem." *Wall Street Journal* (October 25–26, 2008): A11.

Ng, Chiew Leng, Viral Jhaveri, and Ron Graziano. 2006. "HOLT Taiwan: Accounting for Employee Stock Bonus." Credit Suisse HOLT research report (December 5, 2006).

Nonaka, Ikujiro, Ryoko Toyama, and Toru Hirata. 2008. *Managing Flow: A Process Theory of the Knowledge-Based Firm*. New York: Palgrave Macmillan.

North, Douglass C. 1990. *Institutions, Institutional Change and Economic Performance*. Cambridge, UK: Cambridge University Press.

North, Douglass C. 2005. *Understanding the Process of Economic Change*. Princeton, NJ: Princeton University Press, p. 83.

Nulty, Peter. 1994. "Kodak Grabs for Growth Again." *Fortune* (May 16, 1994).

Olson, James M., Neal J. Roese, and Mark P. Zanna. 1996. "Expectancies." In E. Tory Higgins and Arie W. Kruglanski, eds., *Social Psychology: Handbook of Basic Principles*. New York: Guildford Press.

Osinga, Frans P. B. 2007. *Science, Strategy and War: The Strategic Theory of John Boyd*. New York: Routledge.

Perkins, Tom. 2007. "The 'Compliance' Board." *Wall Street Journal* (March 2): A11.

Pfeffer, Jeffrey, and Robert I. Sutton. 2000. *The Knowing–Doing Gap: How Smart Companies Turn Knowledge into Action*. Boston: Harvard Business School Press.

Phelps, Edmund S. 2008, May. "Dynamism and Inclusion: What? Why? How?" Working paper, Center on Capitalism and Society, Columbia University.

Powers, William T. 1998. *Making Sense of Behavior: The Meaning of Control*. New Canaan, CT: Benchmark Publications.

Powers, William T. 2005. *Behavior: The Control of Perception*, 2nd ed. New Canaan: Benchmark Publications.

Powers, William T. 2008. *Living Control Systems III: The Fact of Control*. New Canaan, CT: Benchmark Publications.

Rajan, Raghuran G., and Luigi Zingales. 2003. *Saving Capitalism from the Capitalists*. New York: Crown Business.

Ribstein, Larry L., and Henry N. Butler. 2008. "Where Was SOX?" *Forbes* (December 27, 2008): 28.

Romer, Paul M. 1994. "The Origins of Endogenous Growth." *Journal of Economic Perspectives* 8(1, Winter): 3–32.

Rose, Dwight C. 1928. *Scientific Approach to Investment Management*. New York: Harper & Brothers.

Rutledge, John. 2008. *Lessons from a Road Warrior*. Rutledge Research.

Samuels, Gary. 1996. "Follow the Cash: HOLT Value Associates Hated Wal-Mart in 1991; Its Unique Valuation System Tells HOLT to Love Wal-Mart Now." *Forbes* (September 9, 1996).

Schein, Edgar H. 2003. *DEC Is Dead Long Live DEC: The Lasting Legacy of Digital Equipment Corporation*. San Francisco: Berrett-Koehler.

Schumpeter, Joseph A. 1950. *Capitalism, Socialism and Democracy*, 3rd ed. New York: Harper & Row.

Shimokawa, Koichi, and Takahiro Fujimoto, eds. 2009. *The Birth of Lean: Conversations with Taiichi Ohno, Eiji Toyoda, and Other Figures Who Shaped Toyota Management*. Cambridge, MA: Lean Enterprise Institute.

Shook, John. 2008. *Managing to Learn: Using the A3 Management Process to Solve Problems, Gain Agreement, Mentor, and Lead*. Cambridge, MA: Lean Enterprise Institute.

Sialm, Clemens. 2006, March. "Investment Taxes and Equity Returns." NBER working paper no. 12146.

Sowell, Thomas. 2004. *Applied Economics: Thinking Beyond Stage One.* New York: Basic Books.

Spear, Steven, and H. Kent Bowen. 1999. "Decoding the DNA of the Toyota Production System." *Harvard Business Review* (September/October).

Stalk, George Jr., and Thomas M. Hout. 1990. *Competing Against Time: How Time-Based Competition Is Reshaping Golbal Markets.* New York: Free Press.

Starbuck, William H., and Moshe Farjoun. 2005. *Organization at the Limit: Lessons from the Columbia Disaster.* Malden, MA: Blackwell.

Sterman, John D. 2000. *Business Dyanmics: Systems Thinking and Modeling for a Complex World.* New York: McGraw-Hill Irwin.

Stern, Erik, and Mike Hutchinson. 2004. *The Value Mindset: Returning to the First Principles of Capitalist Enterprise.* Hoboken, NJ: John Wiley & Sons.

Stewart III, G. Bennett. 1994. "EVA: Fact and Fantasy." *Journal of Applied Corporate Finance* 7(2, Summer): 71–84.

Stigler, George. 1963. *Capital and Rates of Return in Manufacturing Industries.* Princeton, NJ: Princeton University Press, p. 54.

Strohmeyer, John. 1986. *Crisis in Bethlehem: Big Steel's Struggle to Survive.* Bethesda, MD: Adler & Adler.

Thaler, Richard H. 2005. *Advances in Behavioral Finance, Volume II,* Princeton, NJ: Princeton University Press.

Thomas, Rawley, and Robert J. Atra. 2009. "The LifeCycle Returns Valuation System." In Benton Gup and Rawley Thomas, eds. *The Valuation Handbook.* Hoboken, NJ: John Wiley & Sons.

Turner, Marcia Layton. 2003. *Kmart's Ten Deadly Sins: How Incompetence Tainted an American Icon.* Hoboken, NJ: John Wiley & Sons.

Ubelhart, Mark C. 2007. "Human Capital Metrics and Analytics: On the Way Toward Standardized Reporting." At www.evidencebasedmanagement.com /guests/ubelhart_jan07.html.

Weick, Karl, and Kathleen Sutcliffe. 2001. *Managing the Unexpected: Assuring High Performance in an Age of Complexity.* San Francisco: Jossey-Bass.

Wiggins, Robern R., and Timothy W. Ruefli. 2005. "Schumpeter's Ghost: Is Hypercompetition Making the Best of Times Shorter?" *Strategic Management Journal* 26(10); 887–911.

Womack, James P., and Daniel T. Jones. 2003. *Lean Thinking: Banish Waste and Create Wealth in Your Corporation,* 2nd ed. New York: Free Press.

Womack, James P., and Daniel T. Jones. 2005. *Lean Solutions: How Companies and Customers Can Create Value and Wealth Together.* New York: Free Press.

Womack, James P., Daniel T. Jones, and Daniel Ross. 1990. *The Machine That Changed the World.* New York: Rawson Macmillan.

Young, Jeffrey S., and William L. Simon. 2005. *Icon: Steve Jobs—The Greatest Second Act in the History of Business.* Hoboken, NJ: John Wiley & Sons.

Zaffron, Steve, and Dave Logan. 2009. *The Three Laws of Performance: Rewriting the Future of Your Organization and Your Life.* San Francisco: Jossey-Bass.

Bartley J. Madden is an independent researcher whose current focus is on market-based solutions to public policy issues. He has written extensively about a proposed dual-track system to circumvent the FDA's monopoly on access to not-yet-approved drugs and to enable patients and doctors to make informed decisions on the use of such drugs. His Shareholder Value Review proposal to improve both corporate governance and the long-term performance of companies is explained in this book. His professional career began with engineering work followed by an MBA at the University of California at Berkeley. In 1969, he co-founded Callard, Madden & Associates in order to develop a more useful valuation framework for both institutional money managers and corporate managements. His research was instrumental in developing the CFROI life-cycle valuation model widely used by many large money management firms today. After managing portfolios for Harbor Capital Advisors, he became a partner at HOLT Value Associates in the early 1990s, a firm created to commercialize the CFROI framework worldwide. His book, *CFROI Valuation: A Total System Approach to Valuing the Firm,* was published by Butterworth-Heinemann in 1999. Credit Suisse acquired HOLT in 2002. Since retiring as a managing director at Credit Suisse, he has published a variety of journal articles and monographs that can be accessed on his web site, www.LearningWhatWorks.com.

A

A3 report, 116, 117
Accountability, 138, 141, 151. *See also* Corporate governance
Accounting
  fair value issues, 99–101
  and life-cycle valuation model, 96, 128
  and use of SVR, 139
Actions and consequences
  and lean thinking, 115, 116
  and PAK Loop, 3, 7, 10, 16, 42, 115, 116
AIG, 24
Ames, Adelbert, Jr., 5
Ames Demonstrations, 5
Annual reports, 132, 141
Anomalies, 95, 96, 105
Apple Computer, 9, 51, 59, 61, 62, 111
Assumptions, 2
Authentic Leadership (George), 71
Autopilot, acting on, 4

B

Baumol, William, 29–31, 38, 43
Bear Stearns, 24
Behavioral finance, 80, 81, 95
Beta, 91, 92, 105, 136
Bethlehem Steel, 15, 51, 62–65, 75, 139
Bhidé, Amar, 50
Board of directors

and corporate governance, 123–127
as facilitator of wealth creation, 130
ineffective oversight by, 43
Lehman Brothers, 125, 126
objections to use of SVR, 138–140
retention of underperforming CEOs, 42, 125
and Shareholder Value Review (SVR), 130–141, 151
standards of performance, 127, 128
Bogle, John, 24
Bonds, 47, 89
Bookstaber, Richard, 25, 26
Bowen, H. Kent, 109
Boyd, John, 14, 15
Brazil, 41
Brown, Tim, 8
Business history, 46, 47, 76. *See also* Life-cycle track records
Business managers and systems thinking, 143, 146–148. *See also* Systems mindset
Business strategy, 112
Business unit analyses, 132, 137, 138
Business-as-usual mindset, 49, 51, 52, 63, 67

C

Callard, Chuck, 80
Callard, Madden & Associates (CMA), 80, 82, 83, 93

Cantril, Hadley, 1, 3
Capital
    competition for, 40
    cost of. *See* Cost of capital
    defined, 36
Capital asset pricing model
    (CAPM), 89, 91, 92, 95, 103,
    105, 136
Capital base, 36
Capitalism. *See* Free-market
    capitalism
Cash flow wind-down,
    84–86
Cash-flow-return-on-investment
    (CFROI). *See* CFROI
Cause and effect, 2–4, 6, 7, 9,
    10, 14, 16, 17, 114,
    115, 143
CFROI (cash-flow-return-on-
    investment)
    described, 51
    and life-cycle valuation model,
    80, 81, 84, 85, 87–91, 93, 94,
    97, 99, 102
    and Shareholder Value Review,
    136
*CFROI Valuation: A Total System
    Approach to Valuing the Firm*
    (Madden), 81
Challenger space shuttle, 6
Chief executive officers (CEOs)
    compensation. *See* Executive
    compensation
    and corporate governance,
    124, 125
    objections to use of SVR,
    138–140
    standard of performance,
    127, 128
    underperforming, 20, 42, 43, 125
Citigroup, 24

CMA. *See* Callard, Madden &
    Associates (CMA)
Collateralized debt obligations
    (CDOs), 145
Collins, Jim, 71
Columbia space shuttle, 6, 7
Command-and-control hierarchy,
    109, 114, 116, 121, 124
Compensation. *See* Executive
    compensation
Competition, 37–43
Competitive advantage, 47, 124,
    136, 137, 146
Competitive life-cycle framework
    Apple Computer, 51, 59, 61, 62
    Bethlehem Steel, 51, 62–65, 75
    described, 45–47
    Digital Equipment Corporation
    (DEC), 51, 58–60, 76
    Donaldson Company, 51, 73–75
    Eastman Kodak, 51, 53–55, 62
    and economic dynamism, 49, 50
    IBM, 51, 55–57, 62, 76
    Kmart, 51, 67–69
    life-cycle track records, 47, 51,
    59, 75–77
    and life-cycle valuation model,
    93, 94
    Medtronic, 51, 69–71
    Nucor, 51, 63, 65, 66
    stages of competitive life-cycle,
    47–49
    and stock prices, 45, 46, 75, 76
    Walgreen Company, 51, 71–73
Consumer wants, 36, 39,
    41, 111
Consumer wealth, 31, 32
Continuous improvement process,
    93–96, 124, 128, 141
Control systems, 16
Copeland, Tom, 102

Corporate culture, 124, 127–130,
    132, 134–137, 141, 146
Corporate earnings, short-term, 21.
    See also Quarterly earnings
Corporate governance
    Eisai Co., Ltd. example, 128–131
    key ideas, summary of, 141
    market-based approach to, 43
    problems with, 124–127
    Shareholder Value Review (SVR),
        123, 130–141, 151
    standard of performance for
        boards, 127, 128
    systems view, 123, 124
Correlation and causality, 15, 16
Cost accounting, 46, 111, 114
Cost of capital
    and competitive life-cycle, 47–49,
        51, 52, 56, 59, 67, 73, 77
    in life-cycle charts, 51, 52
    and life-cycle valuation model,
        81, 83, 88, 91, 92, 94, 100,
        102, 104
    and Shareholder Value Review,
        134–137, 139, 151
    in warranted value calculation,
        47, 149
Creative destruction, 48
Credit default swaps (CDSs), 24
Credit Suisse, 81
Credit Suisse HOLT, 81, 90,
    91, 93
Customers, focus on, 110, 111

D
Danaher Business System
    (DBS), 118
Danaher Corporation, 107, 118, 119
DEC Is Dead, Long Live DEC
    (Schein), 58
Deflation, 86–88

DeLuzio, Mark, 118, 119
A Demon of Our Own Design
    (Bookstaber), 25, 26
Depreciation, 85, 86, 93,
    100, 103
Design firms, 146, 147
Dewey, John, 5
Digital Equipment Corporation
    (DEC), 11, 51, 58–60, 76
Discounted cash flow (DCF), 47,
    80, 81, 87, 91, 105
Diversity, 12, 50, 75
Donaldson, Gordon, 132, 135
Donaldson Company, 51,
    73–75
Drucker, Peter, 143

E
Eastman, George, 53
Eastman Kodak, 51, 53–55,
    62, 111
Economic assets, 135, 136
Economic dynamism, 49, 50
Economic returns
    and competitive life-cycle, 46–49,
        51, 52, 73, 76, 77
    and cost of capital, 151
    and life-cycle valuation model,
        80, 82, 83, 86, 87, 89, 92, 96,
        99–104
    and Shareholder Value Review,
        134–137, 139, 140, 151
    in warranted value calculation,
        82, 149
Economic value added (EVA),
    92, 103
Efficiency, 37–39, 41, 45, 46
Efficient markets, 80, 81, 91, 95
Eisai Co., Ltd., 128–130
Eisner, Michael, 126
Employee stock bonuses, 90, 91

Employees
  as consumers, 39, 40
  incentives, 109
  problem-solving skills, 42, 112,
    114, 121, 146
Entrepreneurs, 30, 31
Erhard, Werner, 129
Ethical behavior, 127
Evolution of organizational
    systems, 12
Executive compensation
  and corporate governance,
    124–126, 128, 134
  and free-market system, 20
  golden parachutes, 20, 42
  and risk management, 27
  underperforming CEOs, 42, 125
Expertise, deference to, 11, 12
Extensible Business Reporting
    Language (XBRL), 101, 105,
    140, 144, 145

F
Fade rate
  and competitive life-cycle, 48, 49,
    52, 59, 62, 76, 77
  and life-cycle valuation model,
    82, 87, 89, 92–94, 96, 97, 99,
    101, 104
  and Shareholder Value Review,
    135–137
  in warranted value calculation,
    82, 149
Failure, preoccupation with, 11
Fair value accounting, 99–101
FedEx, 40
Feedback
  and lean thinking, 116, 117
  loops, 1
  perceiving-acting-knowing (PAK)
    Loop, 3, 8–12, 15
Fiume, Orest, 107, 112

Flexibility in problem solving, 109
Flow, 111, 112, 119, 128
Forrester, Jay W., 1
Free-market capitalism
  and cause-and-effect lags, 42
  competition, 38, 41–43
  components of free-market
    system, 36–39
  consumer wealth and producer
    wealth, 39, 40
  consumers as priority, 41
  and diversity, 50
  and freedom, 28, 29, 31, 35
  and government regulation, 19,
    20, 23–27, 33
  and housing and credit crisis of
    2008-2009, 19–27, 33
  and innovation, 50
  key ideas, summary of, 33, 34, 43
  overview, 19, 35, 36
  perception of, 20, 21
  and risk management, 22, 25–27
  Shareholder Value Review, effect
    on, 141, 151
  and standard of living, 20,
    28–33, 147
Friedman, Milton, 35
Fuller, Joe, 123

G
Gemba, 114
George, Bill, 69, 71, 137
Gerstner, Lou, 55, 56
Global economy, 40, 43
The Goal (Goldratt), 13
Golden parachutes, 20, 42
Goldratt, Eli, 12–14
Good to Great (Collins), 71
Government regulation
  and free-market capitalism, 19,
    20, 23–27, 33, 35, 36
  and inefficiencies, 37

systems thinking for public policy makers, 143–145

Gross domestic product (GDP), 28, 29, 32

H

Haugen, Robert, 79, 95

High-reliability organizations, 10, 11, 26, 108

Hirata, Toru, 129

HOLT Value Associates, 81, 97, 102. *See also* Credit Suisse HOLT

Housing and credit crisis of 2008-2009, 19–27, 33, 90, 145

Hutchinson, Mike, 102

I

IBM, 11, 51, 55–57, 62, 76, 129

Icahn, Carl, 126, 127

IDEO, 8, 9

Incentives, 37, 39, 109, 148

Inefficiency, 37, 38, 41

Inflation, 80, 83, 86–88, 92, 102, 103

Innovation
  and capitalism, 38, 43
  and competitive life-cycle, 45, 48–51, 55, 58, 59, 62, 63, 67, 69, 71, 73, 75
  as continuous process, 37–39
  and design shops, 147
  and economic progress, 50
  and experimentation, 37

Intangible assets
  fair value accounting issues, 99–101
  and valuation models, 85, 88, 103–105

Integrity, 123, 124, 127–129, 132, 134, 141

Interpretations, reluctance to simplify, 11

Inventory, 111, 115, 121

Investor expectations, 46, 80, 81, 83, 93, 94, 96–99, 103, 148

Investors and systems thinking, 143, 148–151

Iverson, Ken, 15, 63, 65

J

Jake Brake, 118

Japan, 41

Jensen, Michael C., 123, 129

Jobs, Steve, 62

Johnson, Tom, 110, 115

Jones, Daniel, 108, 113

K

Kaizens, 115

Kanbans, 114, 115

Kaufman, Stuart, 50

Kmart, 51, 67–69, 99, 112

The Knowing–Doing Gap: How Smart Companies Turn Knowledge into Action (Pfeffer and Sutton), 138

Knowledge
  building, 9, 12, 39, 146, 147
  and competence, 25
  and creation of wealth, 33
  dissemination of, 30, 31
  propositional versus prescriptive, 30

Knowledge base, 55, 149
  and lean thinking, 108–111
  perceiving-acting-knowing (PAK) Loop, 3, 5, 6, 8–10, 13–16

Koch, Charles, 147, 148

Koch Industries, 147, 148

L

Law of unintended consequences, 8

Lean management
  about, 107
  Danaher Corporation, 107, 118, 119

and employees' problem-solving
skills, 42
key ideas, summary of, 119, 121
and PAK Loop, 108–117
principles of, 108, 128
and Shareholder Value Review,
134, 137, 140
Toyota, 42, 146. *See also*
Toyota
*Lean Thinking: Banish Waste
and Create Wealth in Your
Corporation* (Womack and
Jones), 108
Lehman Brothers, 24, 125, 126
Lewis, William W., 41
Life-cycle framework. *See*
Competitive life-cycle
framework
Life-cycle track records
and competitive life-cycle, 47, 51,
59, 75–77
and corporate governance, 130,
132–137, 140, 141
and life-cycle valuation model,
80–83, 86, 93, 94, 96,
100, 104
and managerial skill, 151
Life-cycle valuation model
accounting issues, 99–101
background, 79–81
and CAPM cost of capital issues,
91, 92
and competitive life-cycle, 46
critics, reply to, 102–104
forward-looking discount rates,
89–91
improvement process, 93–96
investors use of, 149
key ideas, summary of, 104, 105
measurement units, 86–88
principles of, 81–86
Wal-Mart example, 96–99

Linear cause-and-effect
thinking, 2
Logan, Dave, 15
Long-term warranted equity value
charts, 93

M
Managerial skill, 46, 47, 51, 52, 55,
59, 63, 69, 76, 94, 97, 99, 100,
149, 151
*Managing Flow: A Process Theory
of the Knowledge-Based
Firm* (Nonaka, Toyama, and
Hirata), 129
*Managing the Unexpected:
Assuring High Performance in
an Age of Complexity* (Weick
and Sutcliffe), 10–12
Market discipline, 38
Market pricing, 37
Market-Based Management
(MBM), 147, 148
Martin, Roger, 147
Medtronic, 9, 51, 69–71, 137
Mill, John Stuart, 49
Mindfulness, 11, 12, 26, 108
Mission, 127, 128
Mokyr, Joel, 30–32
Mortgage-backed securities, 24
Muda (waste), 108. *See also* Waste,
elimination of

N
Net cash receipt (NCR)
and competitive life-cycle, 46
and life-cycle valuation model,
81–83, 85, 87–90, 92–94, 100,
104, 105
and warranted value, 47, 76, 77
Nonaka, Ikujiro, 129
Nondepreciating assets,
83, 84

North, Douglass C., 19
Nucor Corporation, 15, 51, 63, 65, 66, 112

O
Ohno, Taiichi, 146
Olsen, Ken, 58
OODA (observation-orientation-decision-action) Loop, 14, 15
Operating assets, in warranted value calculation, 82, 83, 85
Operations, sensitivity to, 11
Oversimplification of cause and effect, 9, 10, 16

P
PAK Loop. *See* Perceiving-acting-knowing (PAK) Loop
Palmisano, Sam, 56
Patterns, 6
Perceiving-acting-knowing (PAK) Loop
    actions and consequences, 3, 7, 10, 16, 42, 115, 116
    cause and effect analysis, 2–4, 6, 7, 9, 10, 14, 16, 17, 114, 115
    components of, 3, 10
    described, 3
    examples, 10–15
    feedback, 3, 8–12, 15, 116, 117
    and impact of XBRL, 145
    and improvement process, 93–96
    knowledge base, 3, 5, 6, 8–10, 13–16, 49, 55, 108–111
    and life-cycle valuation model, 93–96. *See also* Life-cycle valuation model
    mindfulness, 11, 12, 26, 108
    perceptions, 3–11, 15, 17, 113, 114
    purposes, 3–6, 8–11, 14, 15, 17, 111, 112

Perceptions
    action based on, 1
    correlation and causality, 15, 16
    and individual assumptions, 15, 16
    and lean thinking, 113, 114
    misperceptions, 13
    and OODA Loop, 14, 15
    perceiving-acting-knowing (PAK) Loop, 3–11, 15, 17, 113, 114
    of reality, 2, 4, 5
Perceptual noise, 4
Perez, Antonio, 55
Perfection, 108, 116
Performance measures, 109, 110
Pfeffer, Jeffrey, 138
Phelps, Edmund, 49, 50
Plan-Do-Check-Act (PDCA) cycle, 117, 121
The Power of Productivity (Lewis), 41
Pratt & Whitney, 113
Price signals, 37, 39
Principles of Political Economy (Mill), 49
Private property rights and free-market system, 29, 31, 35
Problem-solving skills, 42, 112, 114, 121, 146
Productivity, 37, 39–43, 45, 49, 63
Profit incentives, 37, 39
Public policy makers and systems thinking, 143–145
Public trust
    and corporate governance, 123, 138, 141
    in financial system, 24, 25
    and free-market system, 20, 21, 24, 25, 34
    and government regulation, 20. *See also* Government regulation

Public trust (*continued*)
Pull work environment, 108,
114, 128
Purposes
and lean thinking, 111, 112
perceiving-acting-knowing
(PAK) Loop, 3–6, 8–11, 14,
15, 17

Q
Quality of life, 32
Quarterly earnings, 75–77, 112,
124, 133, 134, 139, 140,
148–151

R
Rajan, Raghuran G., 21
Rales, Mitchell, 118
Rales, Steven, 118
Rational markets, 91
Real options analysis, 99
Reality, perceptions of, 2, 4, 5
Reinvestment rates
and competitive life-cycle, 46, 48,
52, 73, 75–77
and life-cycle valuation model,
82–84, 86, 87, 89, 92, 94,
99, 104
and Shareholder Value Review,
135, 136, 141
in warranted value calculation,
82, 149
Research and development (R&D),
50, 75, 83, 85, 88, 100, 101,
118, 136, 140
Resilience, commitment to, 11
Resource allocation, 37, 46, 59,
67, 147
Return on net assets (RONA), 85,
88, 104, 136

Return-on-investment (ROI), 47,
48, 51, 87, 88, 102, 104
Risk adjustment, 89, 105
Risk management
and housing and credit crisis of
2008-2009, 22, 23
unknown risks, 25–27
RONA (return on net assets), 85,
88, 104, 136
Rule of law and free-market system,
29, 31, 35

S
Sarbanes-Oxley (SOX), 144
*Saving Capitalism from the
Capitalists* (Rajan and
Zingales), 21
Schein, Edward, 58, 59
Scherr, Allan, 129
Schumpeter, Joseph, 48–50
*The Science of Success: How
Market-Based Management
Built the World's Largest
Private Company* (Koch),
147, 148
Shareholder activists, 126, 127
Shareholder value, 127, 137. *See
also* Shareholder Value Review
(SVR)
Shareholder Value Review (SVR)
benefits of, 140
business unit analyses, 137, 138
components of, 132
described, 130, 132
institutional shareholders,
predicted response from, 151
objections, responding to,
138–140
valuation model selection, 133–135
value-relevant track record,
135–137

Simulation, 88
Spear, Steven, 109
Specialization, 37, 39
Stages of competitive life-cycle, 47–49
Standard of living, 20, 28–33, 41, 147
Standard of performance for boards, 127, 128
Standardization, 109, 116, 146
Stern, Erik, 102
Stewart, Bennett, 102
Stigler, George, 45
Stocks
  discount rates, 89, 90
  market value, 47, 76, 77
  prices, 45, 46, 75, 76, 149–151
Subprime mortgages, 21–23
Sutcliffe, Kathleen, 10–12
Sutton, Robert, 138
SVR. *See* Shareholder Value Review (SVR)
Systems mindset
  causality, 15, 16
  and complex problems, 2
  and corporate governance, 123, 124. *See also* Corporate governance
  correlation, 15, 16
  key ideas, summary of, 17
  and lean thinking, 108, 112, 113, 115, 116, 119, 121
  linear cause-and-effect thinking, 2
  need for examining, 1, 2
  perceiving-acting-knowing (PAK) Loop, 3–17
  and reliable knowledge, 2
  systems thinking, example of, 10–15
  value of, 143

T
Tax rates, 40
Theory of Constraints (Goldratt), 13, 14
Toyama, Ryoko, 129
Toyota, 42, 107–109, 112, 114–117, 121, 146, 147
Track records. *See* Life-cycle track records
Transparency, 132, 133, 138, 141, 145, 151. *See also* Corporate governance
Trust. *See* Public trust

U
United Technologies, 113

V
Valuation models. *See also* Life-cycle valuation model
  earnings-centric, 133, 134, 140, 141, 149
  and Shareholder Value Review, 132–135
  and short-term changes in stock prices, 149
Value specification, 108, 110, 111, 128
Value stream, 108, 113, 114, 116, 119, 121, 128
Voluntary exchange, 36, 37, 39

W
Walgreen, Charles R., III ("Cork"), 71, 73
Walgreen Company, 51, 71–73
Wal-Mart, 41, 67, 69, 73, 96–99
Walt Disney Company, 126
Walton, Sam, 67, 69

Warranted value, 82, 85, 88, 90,
   91, 93, 94, 96, 99, 104. *See
   also* Life-cycle valuation model
Waste, elimination of, 14, 108, 109,
   111, 113, 114, 116
Weick, Karl, 10–12
Welch, Jack, 63
Womack, James, 108, 113
Workflow, 113
World Values Survey, 20

X
XBRL (Extensible Business
   Reporting Language), 101,
   105, 140, 144, 145

Z
Zaffron, Steve, 15, 129
Zingales, Luigi, 21